Practise it! SMASH it!

LISTENING & SPEAKING for FIRST (FCE)

Helen Chilton
& Lynda Edwards

SCHOLASTIC

CONTENTS

Practise it! SMASH it!

is an integrated skills series designed to help you prepare for the Cambridge English exams.

This book focuses on Reading and Writing skills in the *Cambridge English: First* and *First for Schools* exams. Each unit gives detailed advice on how to approach different challenges in the tests. They contain a variety of activities to help build and develop your exam skills and there are useful tips on exam technique throughout.

THE LISTENING TEST

In the *Cambridge English: First* Listening test you need to listen to and understand a variety of tasks which assess your ability to identify and interpret cues, as well as distinguish between language which provides the key and distraction.

The listening test will take about 40 minutes. It is divided into four parts:

PART	LISTENING	TASK TYPE
1	Eight short, unrelated monologues and dialogues (each about 30 seconds long).	One multiple-choice question with three options per recording.
2	One long monologue (3–4 minutes).	Ten sentences to complete with information from the monologue.
3	Five short monologues (about 30 seconds each) on a related subject.	Five questions which require the selection of the correct option from a list of eight options.
4	One long recorded interview between two speakers (3–4 minutes).	Seven multiple-choice questions, each with three options.

THE SPEAKING TEST

In the *Cambridge English: First* Speaking test you must be able to answer both personal and general questions alone or in discussion with your partner. You should be able to use language to compare photographs and talk on your own for a minute as well as discuss a wider general question for several minutes with your partner using a set of prompts.

The Speaking test will take 14 minutes for each pair of students.

It is divided into four parts:

PART	TASK TYPE	TASK DESCRIPTION
1	Short interview	Candidates are asked general personal question by the interlocutor. These could be about their country, work or educational experience, hobbies etc.
2	Long turn	Candidates are given two photographs and asked to compare them and answer a related question. Each candidate is asked to talk about a different pair of photographs and they are also asked a short question related to the pictures after their partner's long turn.
3	Collaborative task	Candidates discuss a question with the help of five prompts. This should be a two-way conversation, not a series of individual long turns. Candidates are then asked to make a decision related to their previous discussion.
4	Discussion	Candidates answer questions related to the topic of the Part 3 collaborative task. These questions may be addressed to candidates individually or to both for discussion.

What's inside?

This book contains **12 units** as well as a complete practice test for each skill. The lessons can be used in any order, depending on the areas you would like to concentrate on.

EXAM INFORMATION:
Get details of important features of the exam such as task types and parts.

TIP BOXES:
Read these for helpful hints and exam advice.

EXAM QUESTIONS:
Tasks in theses coloured boxes are real exam questions.

UNIT FOCUS:
Find out the topic, skills focus and part of the exam covered.

BLOG POSTS:
Get help from other students who are talking about *First*.

SMASH! THE CLOCK: Improve your exam time-management skills by completing these tasks within the set amount of time.

SMASH IT! LISTS:
Read these summaries to find out the best ways to approach exam tasks.

NAVIGATION:
Each unit is split into two parts. The **orange** sections are for Listening and the **green** sections are for Speaking.

GET CHATTY:
These boxes give ideas for further speaking practice outside the classroom.

We hope that this book...

will give you confidence in approaching the *First* exam. We're sure that you will find the tasks both enjoyable and a challenge!

1 Technology:

LISTENING

1 Work in pairs. Look at the photos above. What impact can using technology have on our health? Think about positive and negative effects.

2 Read Shona_7's post. What do you know about the Cambridge First Listening questions?

10 comments ▼

Shona_7

Hey! I'm taking the Cambridge First exam. Can anyone give me any general tips about how the questions are worded in the Listening test and what I should watch out for? Thank you!

Reply | Like | Posted April 1st at 3.12pm

life-saving or soul-destroying?

📋 *The First Listening test has different task types, which include multiple-choice questions, sentence completion and a multiple-matching task.*

3a Read these instructions from different parts of the Listening test. Which task type (multiple-choice questions, sentence completion and multiple-matching task) does each one introduce?

1 You will hear people talking in eight different situations. For questions **1–8**, choose the best answer (**A**, **B** or **C**).

2 You will hear a health expert called Marj Jackson, who is talking about the effect of screens on eyesight.

   For questions **9–18**, complete the sentences with a word or short phrase.

3 You will hear five short extracts in which people are talking about their use of Smartphones. For questions **19–23**, choose from the list (**A–H**) what each speaker says. Use the letters only once. There are three extra letters which you do not need to use.

4 You will hear part of a radio interview with a man called Steve Spencer, who is talking about texting and back problems. For questions **24–30**, choose the best answer, (**A**, **B** or **C**).

3b Work in pairs. Read the instructions again and answer these questions for each task where possible.

- How many people will you hear?
- Who is / are the speaker(s)?
- What are they going to talk about?
- Who do you think they are talking to?
- What do you think the context is?

Take note of the information given in the instruction (e.g. numbers, topic, task type) – it'll help you anticipate what you're going to hear.

4a 🎧 CD1 2 Read this Part 1 question, then listen and choose the correct option.

What attitude does the speaker express about the way he works?

A concern about the difficulties of doing his job

B regret about not looking after himself better at work

C anger about not being provided with the correct equipment

4b 🎧 CD1 2 Listen again. Does the speaker mention the words *concern*, *regret* or *anger*? Which words or phrases express the same feeling as regret?

5a 🎧 CD1 3 Read these Part 2 sentences. Then listen and complete them.

One reason for eye problems is that Smartphone users fail to (**1**) .... frequently enough.

Exposing yourself to blue-violet light can cause blindness, affect (**2**) ...., and give us headaches.

5b 🎧 CD1 3 What do you think the Part 2 text is about? Listen again. Which cues are given in the recording that indicate that the answer for the next question is coming up?

6a **CD1 4** Read this Part 3 question. Then listen and choose the correct option.

> What does the speaker say bothers her most about the use of Smartphones?
>
> **A** the reliance on search engines for information
>
> **B** the difficulty people have in leaving them aside
>
> **C** the effect using phones has on concentration
>
> **D** the way people ignore their surroundings
>
> **E** the effect phones have on the ability to learn

6b **CD1 4** Listen again. Which words give you the answer to the Part 3 question? Which other options does the speaker refer to?

7a **CD1 5** Listen to a question from an interview, similar to the kind of question you may hear in Part 4. How do you think this might be rephrased on the question paper for candidates to answer?

1 What does Steve think is the reason why people use technology on the move?

2 What does Steve say about the injuries his teenage children have had?

3 What does Steve suggest about injuries related to technology?

7b **CD1 6** Read this Part 4 question, then listen and choose the correct option.

> What does Steve suggest about injuries related to technology?
>
> **A** They are easily preventable.
>
> **B** They have similar effects to sports injuries.
>
> **C** Governments should bring in new laws to prevent them.

Watch out! The speaker also mentions parts of the other options, but only one option answers the question correctly.

8 Have you ever suffered any health problems as a result of using technology?

7 WAYS to SMASH! the First Listening test

Remember...

1 … to read the **instructions** and **options** carefully, so you answer the question in the right way.

2 … you'll always hear a **'cue'** which will tell you when the next part of the text is about to start. This is your signal to move on to the next question.

3 … you probably won't read exactly the same questions or phrases that you hear in the recordings. Think about **the meaning**!

4 … speakers may use some of the same words that you see on the question paper – make sure you don't choose an option just because you hear a word from it – it might be the wrong answer!

5 … you have **time** to read the questions and options before you listen.

6 … you will hear each recording **twice**. If you don't hear the answer first time round, you have another chance …

7 … and if you still don't know the answer after the second time of listening – **guess**!

EXAM PRACTICE

1 CD1 7 **Listen and answer the questions about how technology in sport can have a positive effect on health.**

1 You hear an ice-skater talking about injury in the sport.

How does he feel about it?

A surprised by the effect jumping has on the body

B annoyed that injuries frequently interrupt his work

C excited by the prospect of better safety in the sport

2 You hear part of an interview about safety helmets used in sport.

What inspired Gino to carry out research in the field?

A He had suffered sports injuries himself.

B He was asked for information about helmets.

C He didn't think the brand he used was effective.

3 You hear two friends discussing swimwear.

What do they agree about?

A the positive impact of swimwear on performance

B the attractive appearance of the swimwear

C the cost-effectiveness of the swimwear

2 **In which other ways can technology be used to improve our health or performance? Discuss in pairs.**

SPEAKING

1

Work in pairs. You have two minutes to find out as much personal information about your partner as you can.

SPEAKING FOCUS
talking about personal information

Exam task
Speaking, Part 1

2 Read Harv3's post. Do you think he's right?

---
2 comments ▼

Harv3
OK, my first time on this forum. First question – Speaking Test, Part 1. This is when we get asked a couple of personal questions, right? I guess this is the easy part, I can't see what you can do wrong here. Or am I missing something?
Reply | Like | Posted June 4th at 6.43pm

---

3 🎧 CD1 8 Listen to part of a podcast by a Cambridge First interlocutor talking about Part 1 questions. Decide if the statements a-f are true or false and correct the false ones.

a The questions are a mixture of personal and abstract. **T / F**
b Candidates might have to ask each other questions. **T / F**
c It's an opportunity for candidates to show how good their language is. **T / F**
d The examiners only want short answers in this part. **T / F**
e Preparing short speeches is not recommended. **T / F**
f Candidates should practise how to speculate for this part of the test. **T / F**

4a 🎧 CD1 9 Work in pairs. Listen and read candidates' answers to a Part 1 question about sport. What do you think the question was?

A
Yes, I do because I want to be fit.

B
Yes, I am doing a few sport every week. I like play football with some of people, they are my friends. We go train on Thursday and sometimes we have match on Saturday.

C
Yes, I do. I think it's important to keep fit and I also enjoy competing, so I play ping pong matches every weekend at a local club and during the week I often go skateboarding after work.

D
Yes, I really enjoy sport. Every week I go swimming with my friends three or four times. In winter when it's cold I go swimming more often, but during the summer I prefer to spend some time outside and I go walking in the countryside and also I do some riding. We have stables near us and I get cheap lessons. One day I'd like to have my own horse but they're really expensive to keep. My dad plays a lot of golf and I sometimes go with him …

E
I like sports a lot. I started to play tennis when I was five because my parents thought it was good for my health and fitness. It's a cool sport. I have also been in several tennis competitions and I was junior champion at my primary school.

4b 🎧 CD1 9 Listen and read again. Which answer is good? What have the other candidates done wrong? Why?

5 WAYS to SMASH!

Speaking, Part 1:

short conversation

1 Don't worry too much because the part 1 questions are all about YOU and you know all the answers!

2 Make sure you get your basic grammar right for questions you know might come up:

I come from Italy and I live in a small village in the north.
~~I am coming from the Italy and I am living in the small village on the north of.~~

3 Don't prepare long, detailed answers to questions that you think might come up.

I come from France. I was born in a small town on the northern coast. This town is called L'Etretat and it's a very beautiful town. We get a lot of tourists every summer and there are some lovely hotels to stay in. The sea is quite wild ...

4 Don't give a short answer but expand with one or two sentences.

5 Speak clearly and directly to the interlocutor. You can glance at your partner to include him / her but you won't need to ask or discuss anything directly with your partner at this stage of the test.

EXAM PRACTICE

1a Work in pairs. Take turns to ask and answer questions about the two topics.

Sport and exercise

- Tell us about a sports event you've been to or watched recently.
- Do you do any sports regularly? Why / Why not?
- What are your first memories of doing a sport as a child?
- Are you going to do any sport or exercise next weekend?

Food

- Do you usually eat a healthy diet?
- Do you ever cook? What sort of things?
- Do you enjoy watching food and cookery programmes on TV?
  (Why / Why not?)
- Tell us about an enjoyable meal you've had recently.

1b In pairs, write another two questions for each box. Swap with another pair and ask and answer their questions.

GET CHATTY
Play a game with a friend. Write a topic on different cards. Take turns to turn up a card and think of a personal question to ask your friend.

Positive thinking

TOPIC
emotional health

LISTENING FOCUS
understanding feelings, opinions and attitudes

Exam task
Listening, Part 3: multiple matching

SPEAKING FOCUS
comparing photographs

Exam task
Speaking, Part 2

LISTENING

1 Look at the photographs. How do you think each person is feeling?

2 How would you feel in the following situations? Why? Discuss in pairs.

- You have been offered an opportunity to work or study for a year in the United States.
- Your friend borrowed €30 a month ago and hasn't paid it back yet.
- You find out that one of your close friends is going out with your ex-boyfriend / girlfriend.

EXAM PRACTICE 1

In Listening, Part 3, you have to understand the speakers' feelings, opinions and attitudes.

1a 🎧 **CD1 10** Listen to three speakers. Are they feeling optimistic (O) or pessimistic (P)? Circle the correct answer.

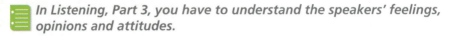

Speaker 1: O / P   **Speaker 2:** O / P   **Speaker 3:** O / P

– way to go!

1b [CD1 10] **Listen again. Discuss these questions in pairs.**

- Whose approach do you think is the most realistic? Why?
- Do you think it's possible to be too optimistic? Why?
- Why do you think it's unhelpful to be pessimistic?

2 **Read the post below and complete the table. Add more adjectives to the table as you learn them.**

23 comments ▼

MaxZ123

Hey – feeling helpful ;) ? I'm trying to complete these lists of adjectives to describe feelings – any ideas? Cheers!

Reply | Like | Posted September 30th at 9.19am

cheerful | dissatisfied | furious | relieved | secure | suspicious | uneasy

Positive	Negative
amused enthusiastic	concerned impatient

3a [CD1 11] **Listen to Conor talking about his driving test. Write down three adjectives he uses to describe his feelings.**

1 .... **2** .... **3** ....

In Listening, Part 3, you may not hear the same words as you read in the questions.

3b **Match what Conor says with what he means.**

1 'I was so disappointed.'
2 'I kind of felt annoyed.'
3 'I'm grateful for what she said.'

a I really appreciate her help.
b My dreams came crashing down around me.
c It was sort of irritating.

3 WAYS to SMASH!

Listening, Part 3:

understanding feelings, opinions and attitudes

1 Make a list of adjectives which describe feelings and their synonyms.

anxious, worried, concerned
astonished, amazed, surprised
curious, fascinated, interested

2 When you hear or read expressions which describe feelings, make a note of them.

I'm not looking forward to the date – what if we don't have anything in common? = anxious
I couldn't believe my eyes! = amazed
I wonder if Jo always behaves like that or whether she's putting on an act. = curious

3 Keep a list of phrases for expressing attitudes and giving opinions.

As far as I'm concerned ...   I reckon ...
I don't know about you, but I'm of the opinion that ...   What's your view on ...?

EXAM PRACTICE 2

In Listening, Part 3, you have to listen to five speakers and match each speaker with one of eight options.

1 **CD1 11** **Listen to Conor again. Which of the questions below does he answer?**

a What do you think makes someone successful?
b How did your instructor feel when you didn't pass your driving test?
c Can you tell us about a time when you were encouraged to try your best?

> Don't rush! Read every instruction twice so that you answer the question correctly.

2 **Look at the following instruction. You will see something similar in the exam.**

Choose how each speaker felt when they were first given some advice.

What do we already know about Conor? Tick all that apply.

a The speaker gave some advice. ☐
b The speaker talked about their feelings. ☐

c The speaker received advice from someone. ☐
d The speaker might have changed their opinion. ☐
e The speaker was given two pieces of advice. ☐

3 **Work in pairs. Are you an optimist or a pessimist? Discuss ways you can be more optimistic when you're dealing with difficulties and challenges.**

4 **CD1 12** **Listen to three speakers talking about how a positive attitude helped them achieve success. Match the advice below with each speaker. There are two letters which you do not need to use.**

a Focus on positive rather than negative events.
b Ask an expert for advice on how to make changes.
c Question your approach to life.
d Alter the way you view disappointments.
e Learn from the mistakes of other people.

Speaker 1 ....
Speaker 2 ....
Speaker 3 ....

5 **Do you agree with the advice the speakers give? Can you think of other useful advice? In pairs, write five top tips for positive thinking.**

SPEAKING

1 Work in pairs. Read the post below. What advice would you give Jacks?

5 comments ▼

Jacks

Got my First speaking test soon and I'm worried about the photograph task. I've got to 'compare' two photographs. How do I do that?

Reply | Like | Posted May 1st at 4.13pm

EXAM PRACTICE 1

1a Work in pairs. Look at the photographs. Note down what's the same or similar in both of them and what's different. Consider the following:

- people
- place
- age
- weather
- activity
- clothes
- emotions

SPEAKING FOCUS
comparing photographs
Exam task
Speaking, Part 2

When you compare the photographs, first talk about what's the same in both of them and then what's different. DON'T give a detailed description of each one!

Photograph 1

Photograph 2

1b Read what a candidate said about the photographs. Did she / he mention the same things as you noted down? Which other points, if any, did she / he mention?

" Both photographs (**1**) *present / show* people who are feeling really happy because they've done something difficult. They've (**2**) *all / every* got their hands in the air – probably because they're proud of what they've done. In (**3**) *each / both* photographs the men have done something physically hard but the man in the first photograph has been climbing (**4**) *although / whereas* the men in the second have been playing football. The man on the left is alone and there's nobody watching him. The men on the right (**5**) *however / but* are in a team and a big crowd of spectators are watching them. The photographs were taken in very different places (**6**) *too / in addition*. The climber is in a beautiful outdoor location – in the mountains — (**7**) *despite / while* the footballers are in a stadium. In both photographs the men are wearing clothes that help them do their sport or activity easily. The climber has probably chosen his own clothes, (**8**) *but / on* the other hand the football team have been told what to wear! I think the (**9**) *most / main* difference between the photographs is that the footballers are taking part in an organised sport (**10**) *as well as / whereas* the climber climbs whenever and wherever he wants to. "

1c Find and <u>underline</u> an example of each of these tenses in exercise 1b.

present simple | present continuous | present perfect simple | present perfect continuous

1d 🎧 **CD1 13** Circle the correct word *in italics* in exercise 1b to complete the candidate's answer. Then listen and check.

1e Use words and phrases from exercise 1b to make more comparisons about the photographs. Use the prompts provided.

For example:
Photograph 1: natural light **Photograph 2:** artificial lighting
There is natural light in the first photograph whereas in the second the light might be artificial.

a **Photographs 1 & 2:** men quite young
b **Photograph 1:** very quiet **Photograph 2:** very noisy
c **Photographs 1 & 2:** men probably tired
d **Photographs 1 & 2:** men look very fit

6 WAYS to SMASH!

Speaking, Part 2:

comparing photographs

1 Don't describe the photographs in detail.
~~A man is standing on top of some rocks and he's waving his hands in the air. In the distance…~~

2 First say what's the same about the photographs using words and phrases like *Both photographs show / In both photographs …*
Both photographs show people who enjoy sport and have achieved something important

3 Say what's different using words like *but / however / while / whereas*
The man on the mountain is alone whereas the men in the second photograph are part of a team.

4 Use the present continuous to talk about activities in the photographs and the present simple with non-continuous verbs.
The men in the team are smiling. They're proud.

5 Use the present perfect simple and continuous to explain what's happened previously in the photographs.
They're dirty because they've been playing football. The climber has chosen his own clothes.

6 Refer to the photographs like this: *In the first photograph / In this photograph / In the photograph on the left …*
In the photograph on the left, a man has just climbed a mountain.

EXAM PRACTICE 2

In Speaking, Part 2, you always compare two photographs AND answer a question. The interlocutor will ask you the question but you can also read the question on your photograph sheet.

1 **Work in pairs. Answer the questions about the photographs below.**

- How do you think the people are feeling?
- How difficult do you think it was to achieve these things?
- What do you think they're going to do next?

2 **Work in pairs. Each set of photographs shows a type of success. Take turns to compare your set of photographs and answer the question: what qualities and skills do these successful people have?**

Student A

Student B

GET CHATTY

To practise comparing photographs, find some photographs about similar subjects online, e.g. on Pinterest. Shut the door and compare the two photos out loud. It's great practice!

TOPIC
personal privacy / breaking the rules

LISTENING FOCUS
understanding different text types (formal and informal language)

Exam task
Listening, Part 1

SPEAKING FOCUS
directing a discussion, turn taking, asking for and giving opinion

Exam task
Speaking, Part 3

LISTENING

1 **Work in pairs to answer the questions.**

- What is CCTV?
- Where do you often see CCTV cameras?
- What is CCTV footage (the films that CCTV cameras record) used for?

In the Listening test, you will hear different people talking in a variety of monologues and dialogues. Some of these may be informal conversations, and others may be more formal.

2a **Work in pairs. Look at this list of situations. Do you think the language used in each situation would be formal, informal, or neutral (neither formal nor informal)? Write F, I or N. Don't worry if you disagree but explain your reasons!**

a a news report on the radio ....
b two students discussing an assignment they have to do ....
c part of a lecture or a class presentation ....
d a conversation between a teacher and a student ....
e a manager talking to an employee in a work review ....
f two friends chatting about a TV programme they have watched ....
g a career's talk for young people still in education ....
h a radio interview with someone talking about their job ....

on CCTV!

2b 🎧 CD1 14 Listen to four recordings. Match each recording with a situation from exercise 2a.

Recording 1 .... Recording 2 .... Recording 3 .... Recording 4 ....

3a 🎧 CD1 15 Listen to four more recordings. Is the language used formal, informal or neutral? Write **F**, **I** or **N**.

Recording 5 .... Recording 6 ....

Recording 7 .... Recording 8 ....

Anticipating whether a text will be formal or informal will help you 'tune in' to what the speakers are saying.

3b 🎧 CD1 15 Listen again. Who are the speakers? Where are they? What are they talking about?

Recording 5 ....

Recording 6 ....

Recording 7 ....

Recording 8 ....

4 🎧 CD1 14 🎧 CD1 15 Listen to the eight recordings once more. Who is in favour of CCTV cameras? Who does not express an opinion? Who is against their use?

5 What do you think? Are CCTV cameras an 'invasion of privacy' or are they necessary in the fight against crime? Work in pairs to discuss your ideas, and give reasons for your answers.

2 WAYS to SMASH!

Listening, Part 1:

understanding different text types

1 When you read the context sentence, think about the situation you're going to listen to, what they're going to talk about, and who the speakers are. This will help you to understand the context before you listen.

You will hear two colleagues discussing their work as scientists.

2 When you read the question, make sure you take note of which speaker you need to answer the question about: you might hear two speakers, but answer a question about only one of them.

What does the man think about his job role?

EXAM PRACTICE

1 You are going to listen to people talking about drones. Look at the pictures. What are drones? What are they used for?

2a Look at these context sentences and questions. Do you think the situations are formal, neutral or informal?

1 You hear a reporter talking about the history of drones.

He is surprised by the fact that drones

A have only recently gained recognition.

B can travel at extremely high speeds.

C have been around for such a long time.

2 You hear a lecturer providing information about drones.

What is she doing?

A encouraging listeners to find out more about the use of drones

B expressing her support for the use of drones in general

C explaining how drones have developed over time

3 You hear two friends talking about the use of drones.

What does the girl think about it?

A that they could be used in place of CCTV cameras

B that their expense stops the wrong people using them

C that her personal life could be affected by them

4 You hear part of a radio interview about the future of drones.

How does the man feel about the future of drones?

A excited by the potential uses for drones in daily life

B doubtful that one particular use will become successful

C concerned that using drones will lead to impersonal service

2b [CD1 16] Now listen and answer the questions in exercise 2a. You will hear people talking in four different situations. For questions 1–4 in exercise 2a, choose the best answer, (A, B or C).

3 How do you feel about drones? Why? What other jobs could you use a drone for? Discuss in pairs.

SPEAKING

1a Work in pairs. Read K8's post and discuss what you would advise her.

---

9 comments ▼

K8

I know there's a discussion part in the Speaking test. Does the examiner give us a question to talk about? Do we take it in turns to give our opinions? Happy for any advice from all you experts! Thanks 😊

Reply | Like | Posted April 20th at 3.20pm

1b Read the answer from an online expert and check if the advice is the same as yours.

ExamXpert

K8 – hi! Yes, your question comes up a lot on our forum. I think this will help you!

First Speaking Part 3
In Part 3 of the speaking test the interlocutor gives you a sheet of paper with a question and several prompts on it to discuss with your partner. You have two minutes to talk about the question. It's really important that it's like a real conversation where you ask for your partner's opinion and interact well. Don't just take turns to give an opinion!

Go to this link http://www.cambridgeenglish.org/exams/first/preparation/ to see some example tasks. Come back to me if you've got any more questions.

Reply | Like | Posted April 20th at 3.42pm

SPEAKING FOCUS
directing a discussion: turn taking, asking for and giving opinion

Exam task
Speaking, Part 3

2  **SMASH! the clock!** Work in pairs. Think about where you are and places you have been today. How many rules are there about what you can / can't or should / shouldn't do in these places? You have **two minutes** to come up with as many as you can.

3 You're on CCTV!

3a Read the task and in pairs note down what you could say about each prompt.

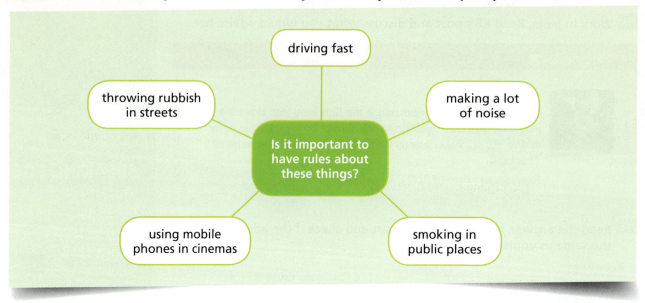

driving fast

throwing rubbish in streets

making a lot of noise

Is it important to have rules about these things?

using mobile phones in cinemas

smoking in public places

3b 🎧 CD1 17 Listen to two candidates discussing the task and answer the questions.

a Did they talk about all the prompts?

b Did they include what you noted down?

c Did they interact or just give their opinions?

3c 🎧 CD1 17 Listen again and complete the useful phrases from the discussion.

a OK, so we _____ to think about ...

b Shall we start _____ this one ...

c Good _____ to start ...

d What do you _____?

e I _____ agree

f How _____ this one?

g How do you _____ about it?

h Too _____ they should.

i What's your _____?

j Don't you _____?

k I _____ agree with you.

l In my _____, no, definitely not.

m I _____ think they need to consider ...

n Let's _____ on to smoking.

o I think you and I are going to have different _____ here.

3d Add the phrases to the correct columns.

Organising the discussion	Asking for opinion	Giving opinion
And finally we need to think about this one.	Have you got any ideas about this?	I feel strongly that ...
We haven't looked at this one yet.	What are your thoughts about ... ?	I'm afraid I think the opposite!
	Well that's what I think! How about you?	I see where you're coming from, but for me ...
		Well, I sort of agree but ...

3e In pairs, discuss the two prompts that the candidates didn't have time for, using some of the phrases above.

8 WAYS to SMASH!

Speaking Part 3:

the discussion task

1 Listen carefully to the question and then use the time you are given to read it again on the sheet.

2 Start by rephrasing the question to check you understand it and to focus yourselves on the task.

OK, so we have to talk about the advantages and disadvantages of ...

3 Use phrases to organise your discussion and move from prompt to prompt:

Shall we start with ... Let's move on to ...

4 Never say: *My turn first. I think this is ...* as the discussion isn't about taking long turns to give opinions but the natural turn taking we do when having a conversation or discussion.

5 Interact with your partner by asking for his / her opinion at different points.

Do you agree? What do you think?

6 You don't have to talk about all the points. Sometimes there isn't time. So you can avoid any points that you don't understand or that are difficult to talk about.

7 Don't worry if you disagree with your partner. There are no right or wrong answers and disagreement makes for a good discussion – but remember to be polite!

8 You only have two minutes for this discussion, so don't worry if the interlocutor interrupts you. He / She has a strict timing to keep to for each part of the test.

EXAM PRACTICE

1a SMASH! the clock!

Work in pairs. Read and do the exam task. You have two minutes.

Here are some things most countries have rules about. Talk to each other about whether it's important to have rules about these things.

- parking
- painting and writing graffiti on buildings
- sharing music and videos online
- **Is it important to have rules about these things?**
- wearing certain clothes in different places
- ordering pills online without prescriptions

1b Look back at the *Smash It!* list above. How many of the eight ways did you manage to do?

GET CHATTY
Practise asking for and giving opinions in English with friends by talking about things that interest you e.g.: what's going to happen in a soap opera, what you think about some news you've heard today, what your opinion is of a new shop or restaurant in town etc. Try to talk about the topic for two minutes – you can even time yourselves!

Making changes

LISTENING

1 Work in pairs. Look at these photographs. What do you think the people are doing? Why? How often do you help people or animals?

TOPIC
lifestyles

LISTENING FOCUS
understanding agreement and disagreement

Exam task
Listening, Part 1: multiple-choice questions

SPEAKING FOCUS
answering discussion-related questions; expanding; exemplifying; adding comments

Exam task
Speaking, Part 4

2a **CD1 18** Listen to some phrases of agreement and disagreement. Write the expressions in the correct column.

Agreeing		Disagreeing	
There's no doubt about it.	S	No way!	S

2b Look at the phrases in exercise 2a again. Do you think the agreement / disagreement is strong, weak, or somewhere in the middle? Write **S**, **W** or **M** next to each phrase in the table.

3a Read this dialogue. Put a cross (*x*) where you think an expression of agreement or disagreement is missing (there are four!).

M Volunteering's a really valuable thing to do in my opinion. I mean, you can really make a difference to other people's lives.

F Did I tell you about my gap year? When I helped out on a volunteering project?

M No – what did you do?

F Oh, I went to this elephant sanctuary abroad, where they look after elephants so they aren't used for labour.

M Aww, that must have been so worthwhile!

F The elephants seem so happy and well-fed, and they live longer and are really healthy. It's so sweet to watch them playing in the water! I just helped out with cleaning and stuff – sounds hard work, I know.

M You must have got a lot out of the experience!

F Did you do a gap year?

M No, but I'd like to do something like that.

3b [CD1 19] Listen and check your answers.

4a Discuss these questions in pairs.

- Do you volunteer?
- If not, would you like to?
- What do you do?
- What kind of volunteering would you like to do?

4b [CD1 19] Listen again and write down the phrases you hear.
Did the phrases express agreement or disagreement?

5a [CD1 20] Listen to two friends talking about raising money. Do they agree or disagree?

5b [CD1 20] Listen again. How do you know when you're going to hear the agreement phrase?

5c Now read the dialogue. <u>Underline</u> the speaker's opinions. Then <u>underline</u> the words
and phrases which show agreement between the speakers.

F What do you reckon about those people who do, like, a hundred marathons in a year or something silly like that – in order to raise money for charity?

M Erm, I don't know, really. I mean, are they doing it for themselves so they look good or genuinely doing it to help other people?

F What does it matter? I suppose if someone's benefitting through someone else giving up their time to help out or take part in challenges or even just make a donation – I can't see the problem in that.

M Sure – though I bet most people wouldn't do something they really hated for the sake of others.

F Probably not!

6 Do you think people really do things just for others without gaining anything
from it themselves? Discuss with your partner.

7 [CD1 21] Now listen to two friends discussing an article they have both read.
What do they agree about? What do they disagree about? Tick all that apply.

	agree	disagree
a how interesting some of the stories in the article were	☐	☐
b how thoughtful the woman in one story was	☐	☐
c how helpful the woman was towards a particular cause	☐	☐
d how difficult it is to ignore someone in need	☐	☐
e how embarrassing it is not to be able to offer help	☐	☐

8 Work in pairs. Read these exam questions. Which of them are agreement /
disagreement questions?

1 You hear two friends talking about 'random acts of kindness'. What do they both say?

2 You hear two colleagues discussing the importance of standing up for your beliefs. How do their opinions differ?

3 You hear two volunteers talking about a project they are involved in. What does the woman think about the work they do?

4 You hear two friends discussing lifestyle changes they'd like to make. What do they both dislike about their current lifestyles?

5 You hear two friends talking about a life-changing experience they had. How does the man feel about the experience they had?

3 WAYS to SMASH!

Listening, Part 1:

understanding agreement and disagreement

BEFORE THE EXAM

1 Make a note of any phrases you hear which express agreement or disagreement. Try to use them in conversation to familiarise yourself with them.

DURING THE EXAM

2 Read the question carefully. Make sure you know whether the question asks you to consider whether the speakers are agreeing or disagreeing.

3 Remember that negative-sounding phrases can sometimes be positive – and vice versa! For example, *You might be right, but …* (disagreement), *No doubt about it!* (agreement).

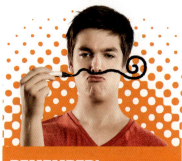

REMEMBER!
Sometimes there may not be an obvious expression of agreement or disagreement (like those in exercise 1), so you'll need to listen very carefully to the speakers' opinions to see whether they are the same or different.

EXAM PRACTICE

1 🎧 **CD1 22** Listen to the Part 1 questions and choose the best answer (**A, B or C**).

1 You hear two friends talking about 'random acts of kindness'.

What do they both say?

A They could each learn from what the other believes.

B It's sometimes easier to expect other people to help.

C Helping others doesn't usually take a lot of effort.

2 You hear two colleagues discussing standing up for change.

What do they disagree about?

A how unfair a current work system is

B how easy it is to speak up about issues

C how colleagues would feel about the woman

3 You hear two friends discussing lifestyle changes they'd like to make.

What do they both dislike about their current lifestyles?

A how little sleep they get

B how unhealthy their diet is

C how unfit they are

2 Discuss these questions in pairs.

- How often do you do kind things for strangers? What was the last thing you did to help someone in need?

- Are you prepared to stand up for what you believe in? When was the last time you stood up for something when other people disagreed with you?

SPEAKING

SPEAKING FOCUS
comparing photographs
Exam task
Speaking, Part 2

1 Work in pairs. Look at the photographs and answer the questions.

- How important are these events to the people in the photographs?
- How will their lives change?
- Write down some more important events that can change people's lives.

2a Read the exam task below and see if the options are the same as you thought about in exercise 1.

Here are some things that can change people's lives. Talk to each other about how these different things can change people's lives.

Starting your first job

Getting married

Having children

How can these different things change people's lives?

Moving to a new town or country

Winning a lot of money

2b

Think about the question and the options for a few moments. Then work with your partner to answer the question. You have **three minutes** to discuss the options.

3 Read Andy's email and questions. Then match Tommy's answers with Andy's questions.

Hi Tommy,

You've done the First Speaking test, haven't you? After the Part 3 discussion we get more questions in Part 4. I'm not really clear about them. I've listed some queries below. Can you help?

Cheers!

Andy

1 Are they the same sort of questions as in Part 1?

2 Does the interlocutor ask us questions in turn?

3 Suppose I can't answer a question?

4 If my partner has a question that I could answer can I interrupt?

5 Should I answer the question quickly or take a long time?

A It depends. The interlocutor might ask you and your partner some questions individually. Also he or she might ask you both to discuss one of the questions.

B Don't worry! The interlocutor has a list of questions and will ask you another one. But don't just sit there and say nothing! Say something like: I'm really sorry I'm afraid I've got no ideas about that! Alternatively you could pass the question to your partner: I've got no idea – what do you think? Your partner's answer might inspire you and you can respond.

C No. In Part 1 the questions are personal and very general. In this part they relate to the topic of the Part 3 question that you've been discussing. There will be questions that ask about your experience and your opinion about different things connected to the options and question you've discussed.

D It's always better to say more than just one sentence. Try to give a reason or an example to support your comment or opinion. If you can develop your answer into a mini discussion with your partner, that's great. Take advantage of a topic you've got a lot of ideas about and have a good discussion about it. The next question might be really difficult!

E If you have some ideas about your partner's question, wait until he or she has finished speaking and add something.

4a **CD1 23** Listen to a candidate answering a Part 4 question. Answer the questions.

a What was the change?

b What was the reason for the change?

c What examples does the candidate give of how it affected him?

4b **CD1 24** Listen to the candidate answering a different question. Answer the questions.

a Why does Candidate A need to make changes?

b What examples does he give?

c What does Candidate B add to the answer?

4c **CD1 23** **CD1 24** Listen again to the answers and complete the useful phrases for expanding an answer by giving reasons and examples.

a My parents moved to France to live .... my dad's job.

b The .... was that I had to leave all my friends behind.

c One .... was that I got really good at French!

d Lots of things! .... I'm not very sporty.

e I ought to do more sporty things .... going to the gym or for a swim.

f But I think I'm just too lazy! .... if a friend phones me up …

g I've got into some bad habits .... using my car to go everywhere instead of walking!

5 Work in pairs. Look at the phrases for adding to your partner's answer. Take turns to answer the same questions as the candidates in exercises 4a and 4b and use the phrases to add to your partner's answer.

> Can I say something here?

> I'd like to add that ...

> I'm just like Paulo

> I agree with Paulo, because ....

> In my case, I ...

5 WAYS to SMASH!

Speaking, Part 4:

answering questions

1 Expand your answers by giving **reasons** and **examples**.

2 If you can't answer a question or know very little about it, say so fluently or ask your partner.

3 If you'd like to add something to your partner's answer, wait until they've finished first.

4 Develop the answer into a **mini discussion** if you can.

5 Don't worry if the interlocutor stops you adding or developing a discussion – it may be that he or she wants to hear a balance of language from both of you and either you or your partner needs to say more.

EXAM PRACTICE

1a Work in pairs. Take turns to answer the Part 4 questions below.

1   What's the most important change you've had in your life? How did it affect you?

2   Would you prefer to have lots of changes in your life or would you prefer life to continue as it is? Why?

3   Do you think technology has changed our lives in a positive or negative way? Why?

4   Are there any aspects of your lifestyle that you would like to change? Why?

5   Do you think television and newspapers can change our opinions about different things? Why / Why not?

6   Do you think it gets easier or more difficult to adapt to changes as we get older? Why?

7   What sort of changes have your parents seen during their lifetimes?

1b Think about the answers you gave? Could you understand and answer them all? What examples did you give? Which questions turned into a short discussion?

GET CHATTY

If you hear people talking about interesting things on TV or read interesting articles in the newspaper note them down, e.g. *A footballer is getting an enormous salary. Is that right or not?* Then ask your friends the questions later in English and see how long you can talk about them for.

5 Soundcheck

TOPIC
music

LISTENING FOCUS
dealing with unknown vocabulary

Exam task
Listening, Parts 1 & 4: multiple-choice questions

SPEAKING FOCUS
answering the questions in Part 2

Exam task
Speaking, Part 2

LISTENING

1 Work in pairs. Answer the questions.

- Do you recognise these musicians / composers? Do you like their music? What kinds of music do you like listening to?
- Why do you think some musicians become more successful than others?

2a CD1 25 Listen to the introduction to a radio interview about singer-songwriter, Ed Sheeran. Look at these words from the introduction. What do you think they mean?

a messy   **b** crumpled   **c** boy next door

2b CD1 25 Now listen to the introduction again and complete this sentence.

With his **messy, (a)**......................... hair and **crumpled** clothes that haven't seen an **(b)**......................... in a while, Ed looks more like the **boy next door** than a **(c)**......................... .

2c Look at the words you completed in exercise 2b. Do they help you to understand the meaning of the words in bold? Match the words and definitions.

1 messy   **a** an ordinary guy
2 crumpled   **b** not ironed
3 boy next door   **c** untidy

3a **CD1 26** Now listen to a girl called Sara talking about Ed Sheeran. Then look at some of the words Sara said. Listen again and circle the correct definition.

a reckon: *estimate / believe*
b gig: *performance / programme*
c be blown away: *be impressed / be upset*

3b **CD1 26** Listen to Sara again and answer this question.

What attitude does Sara express when she talks about Ed?

A admiration for what he has managed to achieve

B envy of the success he has had at a young age

C respect for those who promoted him

3c Did you need to understand the words in exercise 3a to get the right answer to the question in exercise 3b? Why not?

4a **CD1 27** Now listen to two friends talking about things they have read about Ed and answer the exam question.

What do they agree about?

A how well-dressed Ed is   **B** how generous Ed is   **C** how normal Ed is

4b Look at these words from the interview. What do they mean? Which of them did you need to understand in order to answer the question in exercise 4a?

a bunch   **b** auctioning   **c** scruffy   **d** down to earth

4c Now read the text from the recording.

M Do you follow Ed Sheeran on Twitter?

F No, but I like his music. Why?

M Well, he posted this thing about how he was giving his whole wardrobe to a **bunch** of charity shops – and the charities raised more than £6,000 by **auctioning** Ed's old sweatshirts on eBay!

F That's cool! I also heard that he's a clean-freak – you wouldn't think so cos he looks a bit **scruffy**, but apparently he showers twice a day cos he likes to smell nice!

M Hm, you wouldn't think that from his appearance, would you? He seems like a really cool guy, though, doesn't he?

F Yeah, really **down to earth** – not like some musicians you hear about!

4d If someone taking the listening test didn't understand the words in bold, how could they answer the question correctly? What other words or phrases help you to answer the question?

4 WAYS to SMASH!

unknown vocabulary in multiple-choice questions

1 Read the question and options carefully – make sure you know what information you need to listen for.

2 Listen to the whole of what each speaker says to get **the whole message**. Don't get stuck on trying to work out what a particular word means.

3 If you don't understand a word but think it is necessary in order to answer the question, try **ruling out the options** one by one as you listen. In other words, if you know that two of the options are wrong, the remaining option is probably the right answer.

4 If you really have no idea what the answer is – take a **guess**!

EXAM PRACTICE

1 CD1 28 **You are going to hear people talking about music. Answer the questions. If there are words you don't know, apply the strategies you've learned from the *Smash It!* list above to help you.**

1 You hear two friends talking about a singer called Rafaella.

What does the girl think makes Rafaella so arrogant?

A the difficulty of having to live up to expectations

B the challenge of constantly facing photographers

C the level of attention she gets from fans

2 You hear part of a radio report about celebrity.

What is the speaker doing?

A explaining reasons for the way some celebrities act

B criticising those who give in to celebrities' wishes

C evaluating a study into the behaviour of celebrities

3 You hear an actress talking about being famous.

She says that she understands

A how hard it is to remain unaffected by fame.

B that her work has a limited value in the world.

C why celebrities find it hard to deal with attention.

2 **How hard do you think it really is for celebrities to stay down to earth? Discuss in pairs.**

SPEAKING

1 **Work in pairs. Discuss the questions.**

- What was the last piece of music you listened to? Where did you listen to it?
- Does your mood affect the music you listen to?

2 **Read Milton's question and Suzy's answer. Does she answer all his queries?**

23 comments ▼

Mike

In Speaking Part 2 does anyone know the sorts of questions we get asked about the photographs? We have to compare them but then what …? And do both of us have to talk about the same photographs or different ones? I'm confused! Help!

Reply | Like | Posted January 4th at 8.43pm

Suzy

I took the Cambridge First last year and in Part 2 I had to talk about photographs of people dancing! The interlocutor said 'Compare the photographs and say ...' and there was a question – like 'How are the people feeling?' Hope that helps!

Reply | Like | Posted January 4th at 8.49pm

3a (CD1 29) **Listen to and read what the interlocutor says to a candidate. What does she ask the candidate to do?**

> 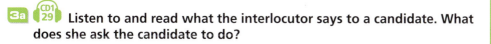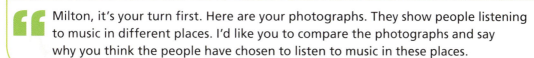Milton, it's your turn first. Here are your photographs. They show people listening to music in different places. I'd like you to compare the photographs and say why you think the people have chosen to listen to music in these places.

SPEAKING FOCUS

answering the questions in Part 2

Exam task

Speaking, Part 2

3b CD1 30 Listen to and read Milton's answer. What does he do wrong?

> As you say, both photographs show people listening to music but they are in different places.
> The first picture shows a lot of people at a music festival. It's a really big event and some
> people are sitting a long way from the stage, whereas the second picture shows a couple
> listening to someone who is playing music in the subway or underground. They are very
> close to the performer and can hear the music very clearly and well. The festival goers, on
> the other hand, certainly can't see the performers very clearly and might not hear them
> very well either! I prefer the first picture because I like music festivals and I go quite
> often. They're great fun. It looks cold but that doesn't matter. I'd like to be there!

3c CD1 30 Listen again to the interlocutor. What should Milton have said to finish his long turn?

4 Here are some more questions the interlocutor could ask about the same pair of pictures. Work in pairs and think of things you could say to answer these questions.

1 ... and say what you think the people are enjoying about listening to music in these situations.

2 ... and say what the people might do next.

3 ... and say what sort of music the people might be listening to.

4 ... and say how you think the people are feeling.

5 Read the interlocutor's comment and then answer the students' questions below.

> After one candidate has talked about the photographs for one minute
> I ask the second candidate a personal question about the topic of those
> photographs. They have up to half a minute to answer. We call this the LCQ
> – the Listening Candidate's Question.

1 'Do I talk about my partner's photographs or just my own?'

2 'Do I just give a short answer to this question, or do I need to extend it?'

3 'What sort of question will it be?'

6 In pairs, ask and answer the LCQs.

1 In which place would you prefer to listen to music? (Why?)

2 Do you ever go to music festivals? (Why / Why not?)

3 Do you give money to street performers? (Why / Why not?)

GET CHATTY

Find some pictures in a magazine or online which are interesting.
Print them or cut them out, and with a friend see how many
different questions you can make for each picture. Who can ask
the most questions about one picture?

7 WAYS to SMASH!

Speaking, Part 2:

answering the questions

1 Listen carefully to the question and if you can't remember it read it – it's on the photograph sheet just above the photographs.

2 The main task question will never ask you which photograph you prefer.

3 The question will always relate to both photographs so make sure you consider both pictures in your answer too.

4 Refer to the question using phrases like:

as for how the people might be feeling ... Now, onto how the people might be feeling ... OK, regarding how the people might be feeling ...

5 The LCQ will always ask for a personal response to the photographs, so make sure you relate it to yourself. Use phrases like:

for me, the street performer would be most interesting, in my opinion ... I'd personally prefer to ...

6 Don't give a short answer e.g.: *I prefer going to festivals.* You have up to 30 seconds so extend your answer with reasons and / or examples.

Personally, I'd prefer to be at the festival because I think they're great fun and it's good to enjoy music with lots of other people. I've been to several and I always enjoy them.

7 Don't give another long turn! The interlocutor will stop you!

EXAM PRACTICE

1 Work in pairs. Each set of photographs shows people singing in different situations. Take turns to compare your set of photographs and answer the question: why do you think the people are singing in these situations?

LCQ: Do you enjoy singing? (Why / Why not?)

Set A

Set B

2 **Did you use any of the advice given in the *Smash it!* list above? Which points were useful?**

6 Inspired by

TOPIC
animals and humans

LISTENING FOCUS
understanding the focuses:
gist, detail, function,
purpose, opinion, feeling,
attitude, agreement

Exam task
Listening, Part 1:
multiple choice

SPEAKING FOCUS
dealing with unfamiliar
vocabulary

Exam task
Speaking, Part 2

LISTENING

1 Work in pairs. Look at the photographs. What do you think these things are? What do you think they might be used for?

2a CD1 31 Listen to the beginning of a radio programme about biomimicry. What is biomimicry? Explain in your own words.

2b CD1 31 Listen again and answer the question.

> 1 What is the speaker doing?
>
>   **A** giving an opinion about the value of engineering
>
>   **B** suggesting the cause of a previous lack of progress
>
>   **C** explaining reasons behind the need for innovation

2c Look at the question and options in exercise 2b again. Is the question about

a what the speaker wants to be understood?

b what the speaker's attitudes are?

c how the speaker is feeling?

3a The question in exercise 2b is an example of a *function* question – it tells us what the speaker is doing. Similar to this is *purpose*. What do you think purpose questions tell us?

a the speaker's main message

b the reason for speaking

c the way the speaker talks

3b Work in pairs. Which of these questions and incomplete sentences relates to purpose?

a The woman believes that copying nature   ....

b What is the speaker's intention?   ....

c What do they both think about the invention?   ....

d The man conveys the emotion of   ....

e The girl expresses her   ....

nature

4 What is the focus of the other questions and incomplete sentences in exercise 3b? Choose from the box.

agreement | attitude | feeling | opinion

5 🎧 CD1 32 Listen to Tegan talking to her science class about a biomimicry project she's been involved in and answer the question.

2 What is the purpose of Tegan's talk?

A to explain how she came up with her idea

B to highlight the reason for the project

C to point out the importance of her invention

6a Which of these Part 1 questions is a) a gist question? b) a detail question?

3 Tegan says that she

A was surprised by how interesting the project was.

B enjoyed the project despite its challenges.

C found the invention project frustrating.

4 What did Tegan find difficult about the biomimicry project?

A getting through the background information

B making her own invention work

C coming up with an idea

6b What do you think the difference is between the gist and detail focuses? Write *gist* or *detail* in the gaps.

.... focuses on the whole message, whereas .... focuses on a specific piece of information.

7 🎧 CD1 32 Now listen to Tegan again and answer the question in 6a.

11 comments ▼

JOD1E

I know there are different kinds of questions in Listening part 1, but how can I practise for it? Ideas please!!!!

Reply | Like | Posted March 9th at 8.49am

8 Can you help JOD1E out? Tick which of the following you think are good ways to practise listening skills.

- leaving English TV / radio programmes on in the background while you tidy up ☐
- watching films in English without subtitles, then telling a friend what is was about ☐
- talking to friends of other nationalities in English ☐
- chatting to English speakers whenever possible ☐
- listening to online talks or podcasts in English and making notes ☐

Listen to things you're interested in. Make sure what you listen to is authentic and in natural English whenever possible. Challenge yourself by choosing things which are just above your level – not way above or below!

In Listening Part 1, you will hear eight different extracts and you have to answer one question for each recording. You will hear each extract twice. There will probably be a mixture of dialogues and monologues.

4 WAYS to SMASH!

Listening, Part 1:

multiple choice

1 Read the questions and options carefully, so you know what the **focus of the question** is and what to listen out for.

2 The **prompt** may be a question or an incomplete sentence: you should approach both of these in the same way.

3 Remember to listen to **the whole** of what the person says before choosing your answer.

4 In the exam, the **topic** of each question will be different.

1a CD1 33 **You will hear four people talking about biomimicry. Listen, and for each question, choose the best answer, A, B or C.**

1 You hear two friends discussing an invention called the robot crab.
What do they agree about?
A how interesting sea life is
B how useful the invention is
C how difficult diving is

2 You hear a researcher talking about an invention called 'Robotic fish'.
How does she feel about it?
A She is surprised by its popularity.
B She is excited about its future potential.
C She is disappointed that it hasn't attracted funding.

3 You hear a scientist talking about developing new ways to collect water.
While he is talking, he reveals his
A eagerness to find a solution to a problem.
B admiration for the researchers' expert skills.
C frustration at the slow rate of progress.

4 You hear two students talking about an essay they have to write on biomimicry.
The girl thinks that
A her choice of topic may be unsuitable.
B she ought to have started work sooner.
C the robot snake is not a helpful technology.

1b Work in pairs. Can you identify the focuses of the questions in exercise 1a?
Choose from feeling, opinion, agreement and attitude.

1c Identify the photographs on page 36.

2 Can you think of a problem in *your* life that biomimicry might help solve?

SPEAKING

1 **Work in pairs and answer the questions.**

- How many animals can you name in two minutes?
- Think of an animal you don't know the word for in English. Describe it to your partner for him / her to guess.
- How do animals help humans in our daily lives?

2 **Read BikerDave's post.**

2 comments ▼

BikerDave

First Speaking Picture task. What do I do if I don't know the English word for something in the photo? Am I going to fail? There could be all sorts of vocab I haven't learned yet. Need your help, people!

Reply | Like | Posted July 12th at 2.13pm

Not knowing the word for something in the photograph won't mean that you automatically fail! The important thing is to explain it in other words or if you can't do that explain your problem in good, natural English. There will be lots of other things to say about the photographs.

3a **CD1 34** **Read the Part 2 task and listen to what candidates said when they didn't know or couldn't remember a word. Do you know the words they couldn't remember?**

Your photographs show animals helping people in different ways.

Compare the photographs and say how the animals are helping the people.

SPEAKING FOCUS
dealing with unfamiliar vocabulary
Exam task
Speaking, Part 2

3b **CD1 34** Listen again and complete the extracts with the right words.

A In the first picture there's a farmer I think with his sheep and a dog... it's a special (**1**) ____ of dog that farmers use to make the sheep go in a particular direction. Sorry, I don't know the name (**2**) ____ English.

B If the sheep are in different places in the field, it's the dog's job to ... oh, what's the (**3**) ____ ... it's (**4**) ____ it runs round them and brings them all together.

C The farmer often has a ..., it's a (**5**) ____ – something he puts in his mouth to give signals to the dog. Sorry, I can't remember the (**6**) ____ word.

D In the picture there's a woman with quite a big dog. It's a ... oh, what do you (**7**) ____ that dog, it's the dog that leads people when they can't see, when they're blind.

E The woman is holding the dog on a ... Oh, I used to know the word (**8**) ____ this ... it's the (**9**) ____ thing that people put round them when they go rock climbing and things like that.

F The woman is also holding a ... oh, (**10**) ____ is it ... it's got fire at the end, sorry ... it's (**11**) ____.

3c Add phrases from the extracts in exercise 3b to the table.

Explain the problem	Say it in other words
Sorry, I just can't remember ...	It's something that ...
I should know the word for this	It's what people use to ...
Sorry, I've got no idea what that is in English	It's what people do when ...
Sorry, I don't know the English word for this ...	It's the place where ...
Sorry, my mind's gone blank ...	It's the person who ...
I'm sure it's got a special name but I can't quite remember it ...	It's a sort of / type of ...

4 Work in pairs. Find some photographs on your phone or in this book with some difficult vocabulary. Take turns to first apologise and then explain the vocabulary item in your own words.

5 WAYS to SMASH!

Speaking, Part 2:

dealing with words you don't know

1 If it's an important word in the photograph, don't ignore it. If it's unimportant, don't worry about it.

2 Don't worry about saying you don't know it or can't remember it. Apologise and say so.

> **I'm sorry I just can't remember the word.**

3 Explain the item in other words.

> **It's a special sort of dog that helps blind people.**

4 Don't get irritated!

> ~~**I don't even know this word in MY language!**~~

5 Don't freeze! Keep talking. There will be a lot more things to say about the photographs that will show. your language skills

2

Work in pairs. Each set of photographs shows people learning about animals in different ways. Take turns to compare your set of photographs and answer the question: Are these good ways to learn about animals? (Try to use phrases from this unit to explain words you don't know in English.)

SET A

SET B

2 **Were there any words that you didn't know? How did you deal with them?**

GET CHATTY

Play guessing games with your friends when you're out. If you're in a café choose something you can see and explain it in English without saying the name and see if your friend can guess.

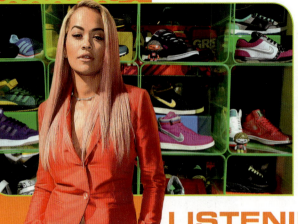

LISTENING

1a Work in pairs. Discuss these questions.

- Name three cool brands. What makes them cool?
- Remember how good it felt to hold your latest Smartphone or wear your new trainers? How long did those feelings last?
- Did you soon start looking enviously at other people's newer Smartphones and trainers? Why?
- What defines a 'must-have' item?

1b Take the quiz.

Are YOU a cool consumer?

1 Describe your mobile phone.

- **A** It's one of the latest models and it looks really cool.
- **B** It's a Smartphone. It's a few months old but it works fine.
- **C** It's a bit old-fashioned but I only use it for texting and phone calls.

2 How many pairs of trainers do you own?

- **A** I've stopped counting. I've got so many different pairs!
- **B** At least four pairs. I like to look good.
- **C** Just a couple of pairs for activities and going out.

3 How do you feel when your friends get new gadgets or clothes?

- **A** I'm always the first in my circle of friends to get new things.
- **B** Jealous – I want to have the same.
- **C** I think 'good for them', it really doesn't bother me.

4 How often do you buy new clothes?

- **A** I'm online every day looking at new clothes and I go shopping every weekend.
- **B** Every few weeks.
- **C** I don't go shopping that often, but I might buy something new if I'm going to an event or party.

5 How do you find out what trainers are 'in' this spring?

- **A** You check for previews on your favourite brands' Facebook pages and read all the fashion magazines every week.
- **B** You chat about fashion with your friends.
- **C** You look in shop windows when you are passing.

Your score!

Mostly As: If it doesn't come with a Nike tick or an Apple logo, then you're not interested. You follow fashion trends religiously, and you wouldn't be caught dead without the latest Smartphone.

Mostly Bs: You know your brands, but you aren't obsessed.

Mostly Cs: You're aware that your stuff might be a bit out-of-date but it doesn't really bother you.

TOPIC
consumerism and shopping

LISTENING FOCUS
predicting information

Exam task
Listening, Part 2: sentence completion

SPEAKING FOCUS
comparing pictures: speculating

Exam task
Speaking, Part 2

In First Listening, Part 2, you will hear someone giving a talk or presentation. You have to complete sentences with missing words. You will hear the words in the recording.

2a What is consumerism? Look at these dictionary definitions and try to predict the missing information. What part of speech do you think is needed (e.g. noun, adjective, verb)? What do you think the missing words are?

Do NOT change the form of the word you hear in the recording!

consumerism

noun **(U)** /kənˈsjuːməˌrɪz(ə)m/

▶ The state of an advanced industrial **1** .... in which a lot of goods are bought and sold.

▶ The situation in which too much **2** .... is given to buying and owning things.

2b [CD2 2] Now listen and check your ideas. Were they correct?

2c Do you think consumerism is a positive or negative thing? Tell your partner.

3a Work in pairs. Answer the questions about each sentence.

a You can use *go* for a place or with an activity. Which one is needed here?

> I go .... every day looking at new clothes and I go shopping every weekend.

b Which letters could the missing word begin with?

> I might buy something new if I'm going to an .... or party.

c Do you need a noun, verb, adverb or adjective here? What can you check on a brand Facebook page?

> I find out what's 'in' by checking .... on my favourite brands' Facebook pages.

d What kinds of magazine are there? Is the missing word a noun or adjective here?

> I read all the .... magazines every week to find out what's currently 'on trend'.

e Which words collocate with *shop*? What can you *look in*?

> I look in shop .... when I'm passing.

f Is the missing word a feeling / attitude / opinion, or a fact? Which part of speech goes with *I'm not (very)... + preposition*?

> I'm not very .... about shopping – my five-year-old trainers are fine!

3b [CD2 3] Now predict the missing words in exercise 3a. Then listen and check.

3c Which sentences do you agree with? Tell your partner.

1a 🎧 **CD2 4** Listen to Jon Marks talking about what makes consumers keep on buying. Complete each sentence with a word or short phrase.

Consumerism

Jon reports that when the new iPhone came out, some people travelled from **(1)** .... to buy it.

Jon says that it is not difficult for manufacturers to adapt the **(2)** .... of products, such as colour and shape.

Jon explains that some products don't work as efficiently after time, so customers buy new **(3)** ....

Jon reminds listeners that **(4)** .... have a lot of influence over consumers.

Jon believes that famous people influence us because of our desire to **(5)** .... with them.

When large companies launch new products, the number of **(6)** .... concerning earlier ones rises.

Jon thinks that our interest in **(7)** .... means we make more comparisons between ourselves and others.

1b Which things on the *Smash it!* List below did you do to complete exercise 1a? Which didn't you do?

1c Do you agree with what Jon says? Who or what is the biggest influence on what you buy?

2 How much notice do you take of advertising campaigns on TV or online? What kind of responsibility (if any) do you think companies have towards consumers?

4 WAYS to SMASH!

Listening, Part 2: predicting information

1 Read the sentences before you listen. Try to **build a picture** of the scenario. This will help you to predict the missing information.

2 Make sure you read carefully – read around the gap and think about which **part of speech** might fill the gap (a noun, a verb etc.). Don't repeat any information in the gap which already exists in the sentence.

3 Remember that the sentences themselves will probably be re-phrased in the recording, so think about the meaning of the whole sentence and listen for the **cues** so you don't lose your place as you listen.

4 Write **EXACTLY** the word you hear which you think fits in the gap. Remember that you may be expected to write more than one word per gap.

SPEAKING

1a Work in pairs. Look at the photographs below. Make speculations about these things:

- How is this person feeling and why?
- What is this person thinking and why?
- What is this person going to do later and why?

1b Write down the different phrases you used to speculate about the people.

2 Read TomTom's post and the answer. Are any of your phrases from exercise 1a and 1b on the list?

SPEAKING FOCUS

comparing pictures: speculating

Exam task
Speaking, Part 2

---

18 comments ▼

TomTom

Hi guys! Me again! This time I need some help with the Picture task in First Speaking. Sometimes you don't know what the people are doing or thinking and you have to guess. I use 'I think' all the time! Any other alternatives?

Reply | Like | Posted December 11th at 6.36pm

Blake7

Hey TT. I'm attaching a list we got from our teacher last week. Should give you some choices!

Reply | Like | Posted December 11th at 6.58pm

SPECULATING...

1 The boy **looks** really worried. *Maybe / Perhaps* he's just got some bad news.

2 The girl **looks** about seventeen. I say that because of the clothes she's wearing.

3 He *might / may / could* be a doctor. He's wearing a white coat.

4 *It looks as if* it's going to rain. The sky is really dark.

5 He's *probably* going to buy the trainers. He's got his wallet in his hand.

6 He *might / may / could have been* running. He looks pretty tired.

7 I *guess* that man is the boss and the others work for him.

8 I *imagine* they've just finished a meal. There are lots of empty plates on the table.

9 I *would say that* they're good friends because they seem quite happy together.

10 It's *possible* that she bought something she didn't like and is taking it back.

11 *There's another possibility.* She *may well have* found something wrong with what she's bought.

3 Work in pairs. Take turns to replace 'I think' in the sentences with a different phrase for speculating from Blake7's list on page 45. How many different sentences can you make?

- **I think** the two people are married.
- **I think** she's ordering something online.
- **I think** they've just been shopping.
- **I think** they're going to have a party.

4 Work in pairs. Do you use mobile phones when you're shopping? Why?

5a Look at the photographs and the task. Discuss what the candidate might say about the photographs.

> Your photographs show people using smart phones when shopping. Compare the photographs and say why you think the people are using their phones.

5b 🎧 **CD2 5** Listen to a candidate's answer and complete the phrases he uses for speculation.

> 66 Both pictures show people out shopping. There are two couples – both girls. They (1) _____ young, maybe early twenties and (2) _____ they're quite close friends because they're helping each other to choose different things. In the first photograph the girls are obviously shopping for clothes. However it isn't that clear in the second photograph. They (3) _____ be shopping for anything really because they're looking in a shop window and we can't see what they're looking at. In each picture one of the girls is using a phone to take a picture. In the first photo I (4) _____ she's taking it to show the other girl what the dress looks like or (5) _____ to send to another friend for advice. In the second picture the girl (6) _____ be checking some information online. (7) ___ that she's comparing prices of things before she buys something. (8) _____ She (9) _____ be photographing something in the window to look at later and to compare with other photos she takes of things on this shopping trip. 99

5 WAYS to SMASH!

Speaking, Part 2:

speculating

1 Use phrases for speculation when you aren't sure about something in the photographs.

> *He looks tired. I imagine he's late for an appointment or something.*

2 When you're speculating about actions in the present use the continuous form.

> *They might be waiting for friends. He could be buying a birthday present.*

3 Don't only speculate about the present. Speculate about the past and future too where possible.

> *He's probably just arrived. He might have bought something earlier.*
> *They might go for a coffee together.*

4 Try to use a variety of phrases to speculate.

> *I think she's a waitress. She might be a waitress.*
> *She could well be a waitress. I imagine she's a waitress etc.*

5 Give a reason for your speculation where possible.

> *She might be a shop assistant because she's pointing at the price of the dress.*

EXAM PRACTICE

1b

Work in pairs. Each set of photographs shows people shopping in different places. Take turns to compare your set of photographs and answer the question: why have the people decided to shop in these places?

SET A

SET B

1b Which phrases did your partner use to speculate?

8 Happy at work?

LISTENING

1 Test your spelling by answering the questions in this quiz.

**Look at these English words.
Choose the correct spelling of each word.**

1 a saftey	**b** safety
2 a professional	**b** proffesional
3 a character	**b** caracter
4 a buisness	**b** business
5 a communication	**b** comunication
6 a attractive	**b** atractive

How did you do? Count one point for each correct spelling.

1–2 You need to work on your spelling!
3–4 Room for improvement!
5–6 Well done! You're a pretty good speller!

TOPIC
work and employment

LISTENING FOCUS
spelling

Exam task
Listening, Part 2:
sentence completion

SPEAKING FOCUS
dealing with Part 3
discussion tasks (2)

Exam task
Speaking, Part 3

2 Work in pairs. Which of the following do you think are good ways to improve your spelling in English? Tick all that apply.

- Listening to the TV / podcasts in English and making a note of new words. ☐
- Asking for definitions and spellings of words people use in conversations with you. ☐
- Learn some common spelling rules in English. ☐
- Avoid using spell check – check spellings yourself! ☐
- Memorise difficult spellings. ☐
- Look words up in a dictionary. ☐
- Keep records of words with their different forms, e.g. past participle, -ing form etc. ☐

3 Which of these techniques do you already use? Which would you like to try? Can you think of other ways to improve spelling?

4 Read Bella.it's post and the response. Then do the exercises (5–8) that JoJo recommends.

3 comments ▼

 Bella.it
Anyone know any spelling rules I can focus on to help me remember difficult words for Listening part 2? Thank you!
Reply | Like | Posted February 26th at 9.42am

 JoJo!
Hi! I know where you're coming from – English spelling's so difficult! I tried these exercises – they worked for me!
Reply | Like | Posted February 26th at 11.13am

5 '*i* before *e* except after *c*'
Look at the spelling rule. Which of these words are spelled correctly? Correct the others.

a acheivement **b** belief **c** peice

d receipt **e** recieve **f** ceiling

6a *-able* or *-ible*? Complete these words with the suffixes -able or -ible.

a accept **b** desire **c** incred

d adapt **e** believe **f** respons

6b Now complete these rules by circling the correct ending.

a If the word before the suffix is added is already a complete word, add *-able* / *-ible*.
b If the word before the suffix is added ends in e, remove the e and add *-able* / *-ible*.
c If the word before the suffix is added doesn't look like a complete word, add *-able* / *-ible*.

7 *-tion* or *-sion*? Match these words with the rules.

collection | creation | education | reception

comprehension

a If the word you want to spell has an ending which sounds like station, then spell it with *-tion*, e.g. *ambition*, *solution*
b If you're making a noun from a verb which ends in *-ate*, then spell it with *-tion*.
c If the suffix comes after any consonant apart from *l*, *n* or *r*, then spell it with *-tion*.
d When a word doesn't follow these rules, use *-sion* instead! Add *-sion* endings to these words: *comprehend*, *discuss*, *permit*, *revise*, *confuse*.

8a Read the sentences and answer these questions.

1 Is the missing word an adjective or noun?
2 Which missing word definitely starts with a consonant?
3 Can you predict the missing words?

a People sometimes say there's a 'glass ....' in certain professions – a barrier to career advancement for women and minorities.
b My cousin in a .... snowboarder – he gets paid to take part in competitions.
c It is simply not .... to discriminate against people of a particular race or gender in the workplace.
d I'm thinking of setting up my own .... making jewellery from broken glass.
e I haven't been granted .... for all the leave I've requested this year.
f My children have no .... whatsoever – they have no idea what they want to achieve in life.

8b Now listen and complete. How many words did you guess correctly?

3 WAYS to SMASH!

Listening, Part 2:

spelling

1 Remember that when you write a word, you often write the correct spelling first time – so if you're not sure, you're probably safer to stick with the spelling you wrote automatically.

2 Do try to spell the word correctly – you may lose points for misspellings. Make educated guesses based on spelling rules where possible – but don't spend too much time on this.

3 Both American and British spellings are usually accepted in answers, so don't worry if you're more familiar with one version of English than the other.

EXAM PRACTICE

1 Work in pairs. Look at the photograph. What job do you think this photograph represents?

2 (CD2 7) You will hear a woman called Sabrina Carlotti giving a careers talk about her job as a travel writer, writing for a magazine. Complete the sentences with a word or short phrase in the exam task below.

Sabrina Carlotti: Travel writer

In her role, Sabrina regularly visits her (**1**) .... at work in the USA to help make the magazine interesting.

Sabrina doesn't always write about exciting places, but provides (**2**) .... for local areas instead.

Projects Sabrina gets involved in locally include (**3**) .... ones.

Sabrina describes the journeys she did when she was a child as (**4**) ....

Sabrina uses the word (**5**) .... to describe both small and larger places she went to as a student.

After college, Sabrina did a course which provided her with contacts she describes as being (**6**) ....

Sabrina can sometimes submit a (**7**) .... to go somewhere, but cannot choose the places she is sent to.

Sabrina says that anyone wanting to be a travel writer needs (**8**) ...., which cannot be taught.

Writing about your local area will help employers understand your (**9**) .... and worth.

Once you have acquired technical and social media skills, Sabrina advises telling others about your (**10**) ....

3 Discuss in pairs.

- What satisfaction do you think Sabrina gets from her job?
- What do you think might be difficult about being a travel writer?
- Would you like to do the job? Why / Why not?

SPEAKING

1 **Work in pairs and answer the questions.**

a In the Part 3 collaborative task how many options are there on your task sheet?

b How long do you have to answer the question?

2a **Read Nicky's post. Do you have a similar concern? What advice would you give him?**

---

3 comments ▼

Nicky 08
I understand that we have a question to answer in Part 3, but what's the link to the words in boxes and how can we make the answer last for 2 minutes? It sounds ages to answer just one question!
Reply | Like | Posted October 16th at 9.23pm

SPEAKING FOCUS
dealing with Part 3
discussion tasks (2)
Exam task
Speaking, Part 3

2b **Read the answer. What do you think she means by 'in detail'?**

---

3 comments ▼

Gottheknowhow
OK! Well Nicky, the words in boxes are things you need to think about when you're answering the question. The question usually refers to them. If you talk about them in detail you can easily fill two minutes – no problem! See my 'Advice for answering Part 3 Question Tips' on our exam website.
Reply | Like | Posted October 16th at 9.46pm

3a **Read the Part 3 question and prompts. Which of the prompts would you start with? Why?**

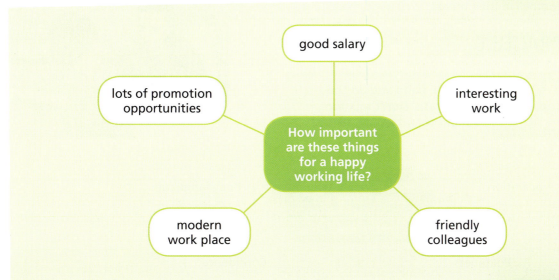

3b (CD2 8) **Read and listen to two candidates doing the task and answer the questions.**

a How long do you think they speak for?

b Do they talk about all the points?

c Do they ask each other's opinions?

d Do they give reasons for their opinions?

e Do they give examples?

f Which word do they use a lot?

A: First, a good salary, that's very important.

B: You're right, it is. What about a modern work place? That's when they have fun office areas and things like ping pong breaks for the staff I think.

A: Yes, and where you can wear what you like to work, not suits and stuff. Mmm. It's important, isn't it?

B: Yes. I think it isn't important to have friendly colleagues. What do you think?

A: No, it's nice. But it isn't always possible. It's more important that you have interesting work.

B: Yes, I agree. And it's good too if you can get promotion.

A: Yes. That's very important.

3c Work in pairs. Read the task again. Note down some points you could say about each prompt.

3d (CD2 9) **Listen to another pair of candidates talking about three of the prompts and answer the questions.**

a Did they include the points that you noted down?

b How many times did they use the word 'important'? What did they say instead?

A: It isn't always possible to be happy at work but it helps if you are, doesn't it?

B: Oh yes – we spend a lot of our lives at work. What about a good salary? How important is that do you think?

A: It depends what you mean by a good salary. I don't think it needs to be very high for people to be happy - as long as it is enough for people to have a basically good standard of living.

B: I totally agree. I mean, you need to live and eat and not have to worry too much about money, but for me that would be enough. Then we've got a modern work place. I imagine that refers to the facilities and attitude of the employers to helping staff to relax and do things like play table football in their breaks.

A: I think you're right. Again – I would say that it would be good to have those things, but it's not vital for a happy working life.

B: Here I have to disagree! I think it makes a lot of difference if you can relax and have fun at work. Otherwise you might get bored or too stressed out to do your job.

A: OK, you've got a point there! Now, work colleagues. For me it's essential to have friendly people round you when you work. They can help make your life easier and make the time you spend at work more enjoyable.

B: Very true!

EXAM PRACTICE

1  **Work in pairs and do the exam task. Don't talk for longer than two minutes.**

Preparation

Politeness

How important are these things are for a successful job interview?

Clothes

Body language

Confidence

2 Work in pairs. Choose one of the questions below, write it on the blank mind map and think of five prompts to add. Then swap with another pair and do the task. Don't talk for longer than two minutes.

- How important are **these things** if you want to start your own business?
- What might be difficult about doing **these jobs**?
- Are **these things** useful in preparing for a working life after school?

6 WAYS to SMASH!

Speaking, Part 3:

answering the central question

1 Look at the question carefully and think about what is being asked and how it relates to the prompts.

2 Choose one of the options you know something about first – don't just start at the top left or right and go round them.

3 Give an example, where possible, to show what you mean.

> **It's great if you have good colleagues. For example my dad's best friend started as a colleague. They've known each other for fifteen years!**

4 Always give a reason for any opinion you give.

> **Promotion's important because if there's nothing to aspire to, you may not be motivated or challenged.**

5 If the question is about something you have no experience of, speculate.

> **I haven't started work yet, but I imagine it would be awful if you didn't get on with your colleagues.**

6 Try to make a real conversation about the topic. Don't just give one or two word answers or a list of things. Disagree with your partner where appropriate – it can encourage good discussion!

3 Which of the things on the *Smash It!* list above did you do in your practice tasks? Which didn't you do?

LISTENING

1 Do you have good time management? Do the quiz to find out.

TIME MANAGEMENT
QUIZ

Are you a procrastinator? An over-committer? A forgetter? Answer these questions to find out how you deal with time pressures.

1 When you've got an important project to get finished for the following day, do you . . .
  A fit it in between tennis lessons and making dinner?
  B do a few minutes' work, then reward yourself by browsing the internet for an hour?
  C search your diary trying to find out what it is you're supposed to be doing?

2 You've got a date in half an hour! Before leaving the house, you . . .
  A try on all your outfits and three different hairstyles before deciding what to wear.
  B ring your date for a reminder of where and when you're meeting.
  C put the shopping away, clean the bathroom, then grab the first thing in your wardrobe.

3 How do you spend your weekends?
  A feeling there's something you ought to be doing but you can't quite remember what it is
  B rushing about from one social activity to another
  C putting off household chores and trying to decide which evening invite to accept

4 You promised to call your friend before going to a party this evening, but you're already running late. Do you …
  A ring as promised, then rush to the party, apologising for arriving late?
  B spend ages getting ready then remember your promise just as you've left the house?
  C send a text promising to ring another time, then decide whether to go to the party or not?

Now circle your answers:
  1 A = O, B = P, C = F
  2 A = P, B = F, C = O
  3 A = F, B = O, C = P
  4 A = O, B = F, C = P

Two or more Os: You're an over-committer. You need to learn to say no sometimes!
Two or more Ps: You're a procrastinator. Just get on with it instead of wasting time!
Two or more Fs: You're a forgetter. Write things down and tick them off as you complete them.

TOPIC
time

LISTENING FOCUS
understanding gist; dealing with distraction
Exam task
Listening, Part 3: multiple matching

SPEAKING FOCUS
dealing with the decision question in Part 3: evaluating; ranking
Exam task
Speaking, Part 3

In Listening Part 3 (multiple matching), you'll hear five people speaking. You need to listen to everything each person says before choosing the corresponding option.

2 [CD2 10] **Listen to the introduction to a radio programme about time management. What is the speaker's general message?**

1 Many people don't have enough time to do all the jobs they need to do.

2 Many people feel stressed by the number of things they have to do.

3 Many people try to put off doing unpleasant tasks.

3 [CD2 11] **Listen to three people talking about difficulties they have in managing their time. Then match them with the general meaning of what they say.**

Speaker 1 ....   **a** I'm always trying to do too much.

Speaker 2 ....   **b** I'm so busy I lose track of where I'm meant to be.

Speaker 3 ....   **c** I waste time doing unimportant things.

4a [CD2 12] **Listen to three time management experts giving advice about managing time better. Write down the main point of what each person says. Then compare your answers with a partner.**

Speaker 1 ....

Speaker 2 ....

Speaker 3 ....

4b **Do you follow any of this advice? Does it help you manage your time better? Tell your partner.**

EXAM PRACTICE

1 **Read the first web post. How would you answer Puzzled_Jo's question? Then compare your ideas with Mohit's reply.**

27 comments ▼

 Puzzled_Jo

I've been listening to some Part 3s in preparation for First Listening and sometimes I think hear more than one option in what the speaker says – how do I know what's irrelevant?

Reply | Like | Posted May 17th at 8.16am

 Mohit

Hi Puzzled_Jo! I had similar problems at first. Just remember that each speaker will mention parts of ideas or words from options which don't the answer the question for that person – make sure you listen for each person's main message! Hope that helps!

Reply | Like | Posted May 17th at 9.47am

Read the instruction really carefully and keep it in mind as you listen to each speaker!

5 WAYS to SMASH!

Listening, Part 3:

multiple matching

1 <u>Underline</u> the key words in the instruction. Make sure you understand what you're being asked to do.

2 Go back to the instruction between listening to each speaker in order to stay on track.

3 Remember that you'll hear each speaker **twice** – so if you aren't sure of the answer first time round, you've got a second chance.

4 If you think you've got all the answers on the first hearing, don't waste the second listening – this is the opportunity to **check your answers**.

5 Remember that there are three options which you don't need to use!

2a 🎧 **CD2 13** **Listen to five speakers talking about managing their time. Which techniques does each speaker mention? Match the speakers with their techniques.**

A	planning mentally in advance	**Speaker 1** ....
B	asking others to help with tasks	
C	keeping a diary of appointments	**Speaker 2** ....
D	write notes of things to achieve	
E	doing challenging tasks first	**Speaker 3** ....
F	balancing hard work with breaks	
G	cutting down on unimportant jobs	**Speaker 4** ....
H	looking for free time to fit in small tasks	
		Speaker 5 ....

2b **Look at the exam instruction and <u>underline</u> the key words.**

You will hear five people talking about time management techniques. Choose the strategy each person adopted to help them manage their time more effectively.

2c 🎧 **CD2 13** **Listen again and answer the question in exercise 2b.**

Speaker 1 ....   **Speaker 2** ....   **Speaker 3** ....

Speaker 4 ....   **Speaker 5** ....

2d **Look at options A–H in exercise 2a. In pairs, discuss which of the strategies you already use, and which you would like to try, giving reasons for your answers.**

3 **Can you think of any other time management strategies of your own? Tell your partner.**

SPEAKING

1 Work in pairs. Name an activity you think it's important to do a) every day b) every evening c) every weekend d) every month.

2 Read the Part 3 task. Did you mention any of these activities in exercise 1?

SPEAKING FOCUS
dealing with the decision question in Part 3: evaluating; ranking

Exam task
Speaking, Part 3

relax alone

contact friends

have fun

Do we need to spend time doing these things every day?

prepare for work or school

do some exercise

3 **SMASH! the clock!**

Read the Don't Forget! list below. Now discuss the question in exercise 2 with your partner for **three minutes**.

DON'T FORGET!
1 Ask your partner's opinion.
2 Extend your answers with examples and reasons.
3 Don't try to rush through all the options.
4 Have a real conversation, don't just give a series of long turns.

4 Read Anton's post. What advice would you give him? Write a reply.

19 comments ▼

Anton

Need some advice! I'm thinking about Part 3 of the Speaking Test. I'm OK with the discussion of the options but then we get another minute to make a decision. Don't you just repeat everything you've already said?

Reply | Like | Posted July 3rd at 7.15pm

Best Answer for How to deal with Part 3 decision question.

Good question! Here's what you need to know.

After you've discussed the options and the question, the interlocutor will stop you and then ask another question connected to the topic. This question asks you to make a decision and you have another minute to talk about this. They call this 'the decision question.'

When you're talking about the decision question you look at the options again but this time you compare them and make a choice. Have a look at this Smash it list!

Reply | Like | Posted July 3rd at 7.54pm

4 WAYS to SMASH!

Speaking, Part 3:

answering the decision question

1 Try NOT to make any decisions in the discussion part – for example, don't choose which option is the best or worst or most important. Just **answer the question**.

2 When you're answering the decision question, don't go directly to the decision and make your choice. You have up to a minute, so say why the others should **NOT be chosen** first.

3 You don't have to agree with your partner! You can have **different ideas**.

4 Don't worry if you **don't have time** to make your final choice. It's better to be talking when the interlocutor stops you than to finish talking early.

5a **CD2 14** Read the decision question that comes after the discussion for the exam task. Listen to two students answering the question.

'Which of these things do you think people should spend most time doing?'

a Which options do they mention?

b Which do they choose and why?

5b 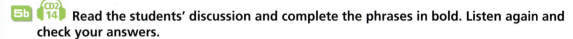 **Read the students' discussion and complete the phrases in bold. Listen again and check your answers.**

Interlocutor: Thank you. Now you have about a minute to decide which of these things people should spend most time doing.

A: OK. So, which of these should we spend MOST time doing? What do you think?

B: That's (a) .... I guess it (b) ... **on** each person. I (c) ... if it's getting close to exams then students should spend most of their free time on preparing. Do you agree?

A: Hm, not really! I (d) ..., yes – that's important, but even when you've got exams, you still need to chill out – like watch some TV or listen to some music.

B: Yeah, **I see your (e) ....** Sometimes we obsess too much about work and then our brains get tired.

A: And even when people have a job, they often spend **(f) ... much** time thinking about work. It isn't the most important thing, is it?

B: No, it isn't! **Some people (g) ... want** to spend a lot of time relaxing on their own. I think my dad would! But **(h) ... me** the most important thing is contacting friends. It's really important to chat to people or email them and share your news and stuff.

B: Yes, and **(i) ...** everyone should do regular exercise but it needn't take loads of time. Just ten minutes can be good for you.

A: I **(j) ... agree with you.** But, although I think contacting friends should take up a lot of time, I think we should spend **(k) ... time** on actually having fun – like going out to the cinema, parties...even shopping with mates! Life's too short to spend it all working or online.

B: That is very **(l) ...!** I think **you've (m) ... me!** Let's **(n) ... for** 'having fun.'

6 **Re-order the words to find more useful phrases for evaluating or ranking options.**

a thing / the / important / is / most   ... to get some exercise.
b the / list / top / of / is   ... to chill out.
c as / nowhere / near / as important / that's   ... having fun.
d people / think / say / that / would / majority / the / of / I   ... contacting friends is most important.
e way / important / more / it's / than   ... preparing for school.
f see / easy / important / the / to / least / it's   ... - that's preparing for work.

EXAM PRACTICE

Work in pairs and do the exam task.

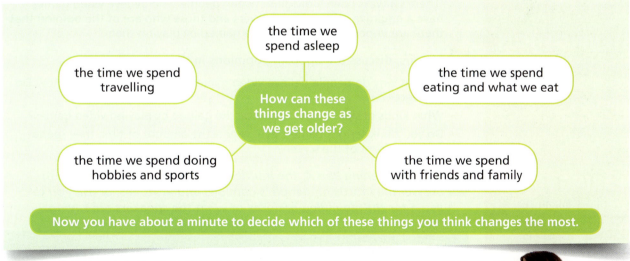

the time we spend asleep

the time we spend travelling

the time we spend eating and what we eat

How can these things change as we get older?

the time we spend doing hobbies and sports

the time we spend with friends and family

Now you have about a minute to decide which of these things you think changes the most.

GET CHATTY
Practise ranking different things with a friend. You could list five places to spend an evening, five TV programmes to watch, five snack bars or restaurants etc. Compare the different choices and give reasons some are better, more popular, more interesting than the others.

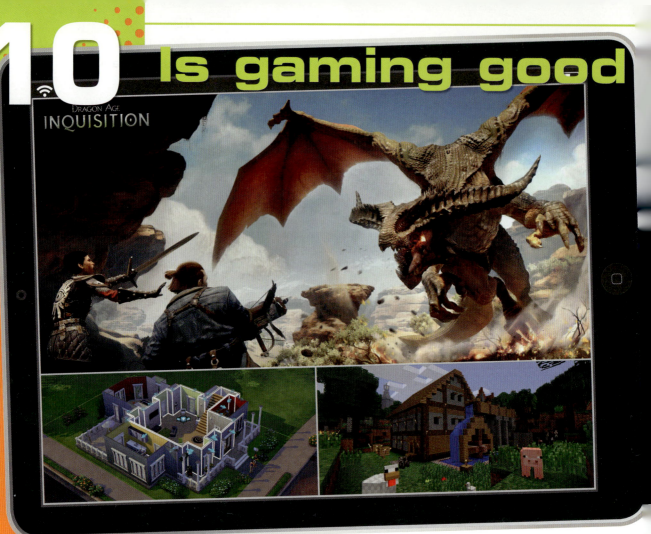

LISTENING

1a Read this statement about playing video games.

'There's always been a divide between people who believe video games have a negative influence on players and those who are of the opinion that there are important life skills to be gained by playing them.'

1b In pairs, discuss the opposing opinions in the statement.

- In what way do people believe video games have a negative influence? Do you agree?
- What kinds of skills do you think can be gained by playing video games?
- Do you think serious gamers ever regret the amount of time they spend sitting in front of the screen?

In First Listening Part 4, the multiple-choice questions you have to answer may focus on people's opinions and attitudes, or ask you to listen for the main idea or detail of what the speakers are saying.

27 comments ▼

Melody

I know in Part 4 we've got to listen for opinions and attitudes. Does anyone know the difference between these, because I don't! Oh, and what about gist and detail? Thanks!

Reply | Like | Posted May 9th at 5.34pm

for you?

2a **Can you help Melody by matching these definitions with ways they might be expressed?**

1 attitude: how you think or feel about something, and how this makes you behave
2 opinion: a thought or belief about something or someone
   a e.g. *I'm scared of …, I'm not interested in …, I regret …*
   b e.g. *I reckon …, I'm of the firm view that …, It's very difficult / upsetting / exciting to …*

2b **Complete the phrases with *gist* or *detail* to answer Melody's second question.**

a Listening for .... is when you listen out for one specific piece of information.
b Listening for .... is when you listen for the general meaning of the whole of what the speaker says.

3a **You are going to listen to a description of the video game *Minecraft*. Read the question.**

What does the speaker think about *Minecraft*?

A It is more flexible than other games of its type.

B Its simplicity is what attracts most players.

C It appeals to different personality types.

3b **Read the question in exercise 3a again. What do you have to listen out for: a detail about what the speaker says, or the speaker's opinion? How do you know?**

3c 🎵 CD2 15 **Now listen to the description and answer the question in exercise 3a.**

3d **How much of the description did you have to listen to until you got the answer?**

4a **Look at these questions about an interview you will hear about *Minecraft*.**

1 What does the speaker believe makes *Minecraft* so popular?
2 What does the speaker express when asked about parents' concerns about gaming?
3 When asked whether *Minecraft* is educational, the speaker says that gaming is …

4b **Which question do you think focuses on …**

a an attitude?   Question ....
b an opinion?   Question ....
c the general meaning (gist)?   Question ....

4c 🎵 CD2 16 **Now listen to the answers and match them to the questions in exercise 4a.**

Answer 1: Question ....
Answer 2: Question ....
Answer 3: Question ....

Thinking about the focus of the question before you listen will help you to understand what you need to listen for!

3 WAYS to SMASH!

Listening, Part 4:

attitude, opinion, gist and detail

1 Read the questions carefully – there's time to do this before you listen.

2 Think about the kind of information you need to listen out for in order to answer each question. The **options** will help you decide this, for example, an **attitude** might be expressed by words like *admires, respects, understands or admiration, respect, understanding*; and words like *believe, think, holds the view that* might introduce **opinions**.

3 Make sure you listen to the whole of each section – don't assume the first thing the speaker says is the answer (though it might be!). This will particularly help you to answer **main idea**, **gist** and **detail questions**.

EXAM PRACTICE

1a (CD2 17) Read the questions. Then listen to the interview about *Minecraft* and choose the best answer, **A**, **B** or **C**.

1 What does the speaker believe makes Minecraft so popular?

   A the focus on the battle between good and evil

   B the freedom of choice players are given

   C the sense of community it provides

2 What does the speaker express when asked about parents' concerns about gaming?

   A approval of their suggestions for alternative activities

   B regret about their lack of understanding of its benefits

   C sympathy about their worries regarding health and safety

3 When asked whether Minecraft is educational, the speaker says that gaming

   A enhances the kinds of skills that are taught to students.

   B provides further practice of particular academic subjects.

   C reflects the teaching techniques used in education.

1b (CD2 17) Compare your answers with a partner. Then listen again to check.

2 Which other skills do you think video games help gamers develop? How might they acquire these skills away from the screen?

SPEAKING

1 **Work in pairs. Discuss the questions.**

- Do you enjoy playing computer games? Why / Why not?
- Some people want to beat themselves and others want to beat opponents in games. Which do you prefer and why?
- Do you think competition in sport and games is a good or bad thing? Why?

2 **Read Blue16's comment. What advice could you give him?**

---

36 comments ▼

Blue16

I just heard I have to talk for a minute in the Part 2 – a minute! How do I do that? What happens if I stop too soon or talk too much? Sounds really tricky to me. ☹

Reply | Like | Posted September 13th at 3.08pm

SPEAKING FOCUS
speaking for a minute in Part 2

Exam task
Speaking, Part 2

3a *CD2 18* **Read the task and listen to two candidates' answers. Write down how long you think each person spoke for. Compare your answers with the rest of the group. Who was closest?**

Your photographs show people playing computer games competitively. Compare the photographs and say how you think the people are feeling.

3b *CD2 18* **Listen again and answer the questions. Discuss your answers with your partner.**

- Did both candidates do what they were asked to do in the task?
- What did candidate A do wrong?
- What did candidate B do wrong?

Use connectors and discourse markers to link your sentences and ideas.

3c Read Candidate A's answer below. The sentences are short and the answer doesn't flow smoothly. Rewrite the answer using connectors and making changes or adding words where necessary. Choose from the connectors in the box.

> and | also | although | but | However | in addition to this | in contrast to this | whereas | which

> 66 In both photographs people are playing computer games competitively. They are in different places. They are competing for different reasons. In the first picture it's a big competition. It's in a big room. There are lots of people playing at the same time. In the second picture there are two people playing. They are at home in a living room. I think they're friends. It's probably a friendly game. The winner is not important. In the first picture they all want to win the competition. 99

3d Work in pairs. Make notes about what you could include when doing the task in exercise 3a using the phrases below.

As you say, both ....
However, in the first picture ....
Another difference is that ....
As for how they are feeling, I would say that .... because ....
I guess the other people are .... because ....

3e **SMASH! the clock!** Take turns to do the task and time your partner. Who gets closest to **one minute**?

6 WAYS to SMASH! Speaking, Part 2:

talking for a minute

1 Answer both parts of the task.

Remember to compare AND answer the question.

2 If you run out of things to say, look again at the question and make sure you give reasons and examples.

> **I think they're nervous because they really want to win the competition and lots of people might be watching them.**

3 Don't worry if you're still speaking when the interlocutor interrupts you. It's better to say too much than too little.

4 Use connectors and discourse markers to make your talk flow smoothly.

> **In spite of the nerves they're also probably really excited and keen to do well.**

5 Don't worry if you don't manage to finish your answer in the time. As long as you show that you have addressed both parts of the question, that's fine.

6 Don't spend a lot of time searching for words. A minute is actually quite short and you shouldn't waste your time thinking but use it to show off your language skills.

EXAM PRACTICE

1

SMASH! the clock!

Work in pairs. Each set of photographs shows people playing games in different competitions. Take turns to compare your set of photographs and answer the question: How do you think the people have prepared for these competitions? Speak for **one minute**.

SET A

SET B

2 Look at the *Smash it!* list on page 64. Which pieces of advice did your partner follow?

GET CHATTY

Practise speaking for a minute by choosing a topic and seeing if you can speak about it without stopping for a minute. You could record yourself on your phone and then check how long you spoke for afterwards. Make a topic list with random topics, e.g. animals, favourite places, hobbies etc. and choose a topic from the list to talk about.

TOPIC
education and learning

LISTENING FOCUS
listening for cues

Exam task
Listening, Part 4: multiple choice

SPEAKING FOCUS
working with a partner; interrupting, encouraging, balancing, asking for clarification

Exam task
Speaking, Part 3

LISTENING

1 Look at the pictures. What do you think these people are inspired by? What makes you feel inspired? What do you do when you need inspiration? Tell your partner.

In First Listening Part 4, you will hear a conversation. This could be a discussion or interview. You have to answer seven multiple-choice questions with three options. Only one option is correct.

2 Read DizEE's post. What is he worried about?

2 comments ▼

DizzEE
In Listening Part 4, I know there are seven multiple-choice questions to answer – but how do I know when one answer's finished and the next one begins? I don't want to miss anything!
Reply | Like | Posted January 18th at 4.22pm

3a Read the introduction to a radio programme in which an art teacher called Sadie is being interviewed about her work.

> " Good morning, Sadie. Thanks for joining us on Art Hour.
> You're a teacher at the Art Studio in the city's Glasson Museum. "

3b What questions do you think the interviewer will ask? Think of seven questions. Discuss your ideas in pairs.

3c Now look at the interviewer's questions at the bottom of this page. Were your ideas correct?

3d Read the questions again. What do you think Sadie's answers are? Discuss your ideas in pairs.

3e Match the interview questions with the beginnings of Sadie's answers.

a There's still this idea that museums are stuffy, formal places …

b I want to make new artists …

c It's a great joy. I've wanted to guide people …

d Sure. …. I'm in charge of …

e I don't have any art or teaching qualifications.

f I hope so! One of the things I focus on is …

g It goes without saying you've got to be organized …

4 Now match the multiple-choice questions from the test paper with the interviewer's questions. Write Q1–Q7 in the spaces.

a Sadie feels that her work is inspirational in the way it ....

b Why does Sadie say that being organized is a necessary skill in her job? ....

c How does Sadie feel about her job generally? ....

d When Sadie explains her goals as an art teacher, she says she wants to ....

e Sadie thinks that some listeners will be surprised to hear that ....

f Sadie says that in her role as an art teacher, she ....

g How did Sadie start out in her chosen field of work? ....

EXAM PRACTICE

1a Listen to the interview and answer the questions by choosing A, B or C.

1 Sadie says that in her role as an art teacher, she …

A wishes other teachers had time to devote to research.

B struggles to gain access to resources for local teachers.

C has the opportunity to share ideas with other teachers.

2 Why does Sadie say that being organized is a necessary skill in her job?

A She has to make bookings for other artists on a regular basis.

B She never knows in advance what her workday may involve.

C She deals with a wide variety of tasks on a daily basis.

Q1 Can you tell us more about what your job entails?

Q2 So what skills are required for your job?

Q3 What are your goals as a teacher?

Q4 Is your work as inspirational as it sounds?

Q5 How did you get into this line of work?

Q6 Is there anything listeners would find surprising about what you do?

Q7 How do you feel about your work as a whole?

3 When Sadie explains her goals as an art teacher, she says she wants to …

    A challenge popular beliefs about the art world.

    B encourage more people to gain qualifications in art.

    C help students of art to make useful contacts.

4 Sadie feels that her work is inspirational in the way it …

    A helps her to improve her own techniques as an artist.

    B helps her make decisions about how to guide new artists.

    C helps students consider how their work may develop in future.

5 How did Sadie start out in her chosen field of work?

    A She asked for career advice from a friend with an art degree.

    B Her interest in art was sparked by a friend's work.

    C She particularly liked some work she saw at an exhibition.

6 Sadie thinks that some listeners will be surprised to hear that

    A today's museums are more interesting than they used to be.

    B workshops at the museum are livelier than they might expect.

    C it is common for art to be taught in museums these days.

7 How does Sadie feel about her job generally?

    A fascinated by the thought processes her students demonstrate

    B proud of having contributed to the success of well-known artists

    C excited by the prospect of promoting the museum nationally

Remember to listen for meaning, not exact words or phrases!

1b Circle **Y** for *Yes* or **N** for *No*.

a Do the interviewer's questions and the questions in the test use exactly the same words?   **Y / N**

b Do both sets of questions have the same meaning?   **Y / N**

c Does Sadie give the answer to each question immediately each time?   **Y / N**

1c CD2 19 **Listen again and then check your answers with a partner.**

4 WAYS to SMASH!

Listening, Part 4: multiple choice

1 Read **all the questions and options** carefully, so you know what to listen out for. You'll be given time to do this.

2 You'll always hear each question **cued in the recording**, so don't worry about losing your place!

3 If you do miss one of the questions, don't worry! Look ahead to the next question.

4 Remember you'll hear the audio **twice**, so you can answer anything you aren't sure about second time round.

SPEAKING

1 Work in pairs. Read the post. Have you got any suggestions to help KerryK?

6 comments ▼

KerryK
For my First Speaking test I think I can answer questions OK when it's just me, but with a partner I may not know – that's got to be harder, hasn't it? What if they speak too much, or don't speak at all? And what if I can't understand them?
Reply | Like | Posted July 17th at 8.56pm

2 Work in pairs. In your family, whose ideas do you most admire and respect the most? Why?

3a
SMASH! the clock! Read the exam task below and think about the question and the options for a few moments. Then work with your partner to answer the question. You have **three minutes** to discuss the options, then **one minute** to answer the decision question.

SPEAKING FOCUS
working with a partner: interrupting, encouraging, balancing, asking for clarification

Exam task
Speaking, Part 3

teachers

celebrities

parents

How can these people influence the way we think and the things we do in life?

politicians

friends

Which of these people do you think has the most influence on the career we choose? Why?

3b Think about your discussion. Did you both speak for about the same length of time or did one of you speak more than the other?

3c CD2 20 Listen to two candidates discussing one of the options. What is the problem?

3d CD2 21 Listen again. This time notice what Candidate A says to get a share of the discussion.

3e CD2 22 Listen to another extract from the same discussion. What's the problem and how do the candidates deal with it?

4 Read the blog post and the useful phrases below.

---

5 comments ▼

Ace the test

Hi there, KerryK! Here's a link to some useful phrases you can use when you're discussing something with a partner in the test. That should do the trick! www. ....

Reply | Like | Posted July 17th at 9.07pm

Interrupting politely

Excuse me but ...

Sorry to interrupt but ...

Can I come in here? I think ....

Good point, but I'd just like to add something ...

Before you go on I'd like to say that ....

When you don't understand something

I'm sorry – did you say ' ....'?

Sorry, could you say that again?

Sorry – I didn't catch that.

What do you mean by ...?

Could you repeat that last point please ... a little more slowly?

When you want to encourage your partner to say more

Yes, that's a good idea. Have you got an example of that?

Great. Why do you think that?

Some people say that celebrities can also influence young people in a bad way. What do you think?

Don't you think that sportsmen encourage children to do sport?

REMEMBER
- Don't give long turns but have a real conversation.
- Ask for and give opinions.
- Answer the question – don't make your answer a personal reaction.
- Use a range of language – don't just repeat what your partner says.
- With the decision question, discuss it with your partner, don't just say what you think.
- Say more than one sentence.
- Answer the question. If you don't hear it clearly, ask for repetition.

EXAM PRACTICE

1a Look at the exam task. Think about the question and options for a few moments.

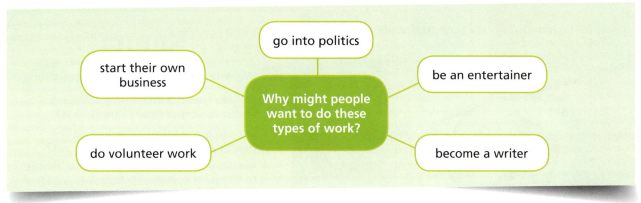

go into politics

start their own business

be an entertainer

Why might people want to do these types of work?

do volunteer work

become a writer

1b Talk about one or two of the options and take turns to do the following:

1 Student A keeps on talking, Student B interrupts politely.
2 Student A only says a few words. Student B encourages him/her to speak more.
3 Student A speaks too fast, not clearly. Student B asks for repetition and clarification.

4 WAYS to SMASH!

Speaking, Part 3:

working with a partner

1 Interrupt your partner politely if she / he is talking all the time.

2 Ask for **repetition or clarification** if you don't understand something she / he says.

3 Try to **prompt** or **encourage** your partner if she / he is saying very little.

4 Try to **speak clearly** and not too fast, so that your partner can understand you.

Advice from an interlocutor!

We need to hear both students' English, so try to balance the conversation.

Students who talk all the time and don't allow their partner to say anything may lose marks because a discussion is all about interacting.

If your partner doesn't say much but you give them the opportunity, you won't lose marks for dominating the conversation.

You won't lose marks if you don't understand something your partner says and ask him / her to explain. That's much better than continuing a discussion in the wrong direction!

GET CHATTY

Arrange a short time every week when you and a friend discuss something interesting in English only. Make sure you balance the conversation. You'll soon get used to taking natural turns!

LISTENING

1 **Work in pairs to answer the questions.**

- Do you spend a lot of time thinking about food and how to prepare it?
- Do you pay a lot of attention to the health implications of what you eat?
- Would you describe yourself as a 'foodie' (a foodie is someone who takes great pleasure in food)?

The context sentence (Parts 1–4): common mistakes

Not reading the context sentence properly. This is the sentence which appears first in each part of the paper. It tells you what you're going to listen to and may include information about

- who's speaking (and who they're speaking to)
- what they're going to talking about
- their reason for speaking

The third bullet is especially important to remember in Part 3!

2 **CD2 23** **Listen to a Part 3 context sentence and choose the correct option.**

a Five speakers will explain how they changed their diet.

b Five speakers will tell us about how they wish to eat better.

c Five speakers will offer us advice about improving our diet.

The multiple-choice questions (Parts 1 and 4): common mistakes

Misreading the question, especially when

- you are asked a question about only one speaker's opinion (Part 1)
- you are asked whether the speakers agree or disagree (Part 1)
- you assume that the first thing you hear is the answer (Part 1 and Part 4)
- you miss a cue because you're still thinking about the last question (Part 1 and Part 4)

3a **CD2 24** **Listen to a multiple-choice question. What kind of information do you think the speaker will give?**

3b **CD2 25** **Now listen to the speaker's answer and choose the correct option.**

What mistakes does the nutritionist think people make when they eat out?

A trying to limit themselves to a strict diet

B believing that menus don't offer healthy alternatives

C eating too much of the wrong thing

TOPIC
food and health

LISTENING FOCUS
summary of common problems with the Listening paper
Exam task
Listening, Parts 1–4

SPEAKING FOCUS
summary of common problems with the Speaking paper
Exam task
Speaking, Parts 1–4

foodie?

The options (Parts 1, 3 and 4): common mistakes

- Jumping for the first thing you hear which sounds similar to an option.
  ALL of the options may appear possible, and you will hear some similar ideas
  and words connected to each option in the recordings, but only ONE option is correct
  for each question (in Part 3, this is one option per speaker) – pick the right one!
- There are negatives in the options – listen carefully for positive and negative statements.

---

4 **Look at the options. What do they mean? Match 1–3 with a–c.**

1 I felt trapped in an unhealthy eating pattern.

2 It never struck me that I could make changes to the way I was eating.

3 I was aware of what I was doing wrong.

a I knew what mistakes I was making.

b I couldn't stop eating the wrong things.

c I didn't realise altering my diet was possible.

---

5 CD2 26 **Listen to a shortened version of a Part 2 sentence completion listening task. What do you think the first three sentences you have to complete might be about? What do you think the missing word could be for each sentence?**

topic	possible key
1	
2	
3	

---

6 **What do you often forget to do in a listening test? What could you do to make sure you avoid these mistakes in the First Listening test? Discuss in pairs.**

6 WAYS to SMASH! the First Listening test

1 Take full advantage of the time you are given to read the question paper before you listen. This will help you to **anticipate** what you're going to hear, and in the case of Part 2, help you start thinking about possible keys.

2 Underline **key words** in the questions. Refer back to these from time to time as you listen.

3 If you miss an answer, don't worry. Just stay on track and remember that you will hear each recording **TWICE**.

4 Listen to everything the speaker has to say regarding the specific topic of the question before you choose your answer.

5 Write your answers on the question paper as you listen – you'll have five minutes at the end to transfer your answers to the answer sheet. Pay attention to spelling!

6 If in doubt – **GUESS** the answer! You won't lose anything by giving it a go.

EXAM PRACTICE

(CD2 27) Test yourself! You will hear a shortened version of the Listening paper. Read the questions and underline the key words. Then listen and answer the questions.

Part 1

You hear two colleagues talking about eating when busy. What do they agree about?

A how much time planning meals takes up

B how difficult it is to plan meal breaks at work

C how hard it is to eat healthily when busy

Part 2

You will hear a dietician called Michael Meadley, talking about good and bad foods to eat. For questions 1–3, complete the sentences with a word or short phrase.

Good foods or bad?

Michael believes that although people generally know what to eat, (**1**) .... remain about some foods.

Michael compares the sugar content in cereal to that of a (**2**) ....

Michael suggests limiting foods such as guacamole because their (**3**) .... count is high.

Part 3

You will hear two short extracts in which people are talking about their diet. For questions **1** and **2**, choose from the list (**A–D**) what each speaker says they want to improve about their diet. Use the letters only once. There are two extra letters which you do not need to use.

A   reducing the amount of fat I eat

B   avoiding sugary snacks at work   **Speaker 1** ....

C   drinking more water than fizzy drinks   **Speaker 2** ....

D   avoiding treats before bedtime

Part 4

You will hear a health expert called Carole Butler talking about school meals. Choose the best answer to the question (**A**, **B** or **C**). What does the nutritionist think about school meals?

A There is misunderstanding about what is good and bad.

B Many menus offer a restricted number of options.

C It would be better for children to take in food from home.

SPEAKING

EXAM PRACTICE

Part 1

1 **CD2 28** Work in pairs. Read the Part 1 question and listen to a candidate's answer. What does she do wrong?

> Tell us about something you cooked recently.

2 Work in pairs. Take turns to ask and answer the Part 1 questions.

- Tell us about something you cooked recently.
- What is your favourite place to eat? Why?
- What would be your perfect meal?

Part 2

1 **CD2 29** Work in pairs. Read the Part 2 question and listen to two candidates' answers. What do they do wrong?

> Your photographs show people preparing food in different places. Compare your photographs and say what might be difficult about preparing food in these places.

LCQ: Do you enjoy cooking?

> **Candidate A:** In the first picture I can see some chefs and they are preparing food in a kitchen. I think it is a professional kitchen. There are a lot of chefs and they are all busy cooking. I can see seven chefs. The chef at the front is cooking something very hot. There are flames coming from his pan. But he doesn't seem worried. Perhaps it is part of the cooking method. It is a big kitchen, so it's probably a big restaurant. I like this picture. The second picture is of a man in a kitchen with his children. He is holding his young child and at the same time he is checking his phone. His little girl is doing something, maybe washing or cutting some fruit. She is making a mess. The man isn't watching her. I don't like fruit so I like the first picture more I think.

Interlocutor: Max, do you enjoy cooking?

Candidate B: Yes.

2 Work in pairs. Take turns to practise the Part 2 task.
Student A: do the task from exercise 1.
Student B: do the task below. After the one minute talk ask your partner the
LCQ below the pictures.

Your photographs show people cooking food outside. Compare your photographs and say what the people might enjoy about cooking outside.

LCQ: Which food would you prefer to eat?

Part 3

1 [CD2 30] Work in pairs. Read the Part 3 task and listen to an extract from the discussion. What do they do wrong?

Here are some places where people sometimes go to eat.

Talk to each other about the good and bad points of eating in these places.

in an award-winning
restaurant

in a school or
work canteen

at a fast food
restaurant

**What are the good
and bad points of
eating in these places?**

a picnic in the
countryside or park

on a train or a
plane

Which of these places do you think is popular with most people?

A: OK, I'll start. It's good to eat in a school canteen because it's easy to get to and it doesn't cost much. But sometimes the food isn't well-cooked and it can be a bit boring. It's also very noisy in a canteen. Also you see always the same people. Also, sometimes there's a long queue because there are lots of people who want to eat.

B: Now it's my turn. It's good to eat in a fast food restaurant. I really like burgers and chicken with chips. It's very tasty. Sometimes I go at lunchtime with my friends. There are lots of fast food restaurants near my work. We often go to a burger restaurant and I always order a cheese burger with fries.

A: Now it's my turn. It's good to go on a picnic ...

2 Listen to the same candidates answering the decision question. What do they do wrong?

> **A:** I think the canteen is popular because the people don't have a choice.

> **B:** I think the fast food restaurant is popular because the food is good.

3 SMASH! the clock!

Work in pairs. Read the question again and spend two minutes discussing the main question and one minute discussing the decision question.

Part 4

1 CD2 32 **Work in pairs. Read the Part 4 question and listen to two candidates answering it. What do they do wrong?**

1 Do you think it's important for families to regularly eat meals together? Why / Why not?

A: That's an interesting question. Today a lot of families don't eat together and I think that's a pity. It's important because ...

B: I agree. In my family we always eat dinner together. Well, maybe not always, sometimes my dad finishes work late and so we go ahead without him. But it's a good opportunity to …

A: Yes. It's a time when you can talk over what you've done during the day and …

B: As I was saying, it's a good opportunity to talk about any problems …

Interlocutor: Thank you.

2 **Work in pairs. Take turns to ask and answer the questions. Add comments to your partner's when appropriate.**

1 Is it important for children to learn to cook? Why?

2 Some schools have banned unhealthy food snacks at school. Do you think this is a good thing? Why / Why not?

3 Cookery competitions are becoming very popular on TV. Why do you think this is?

7 WAYS to SMASH! the First Speaking test

1 Try not to freeze or dry up when giving your Part 2 talk. It is better to say anything – even if you **repeat** or **summarise** what you've already said – than to stay silent.

2 Don't panic if you don't know the word for something, you can always **rephrase** or **explain** your meaning.

3 If you don't hear a question, ask for **repetition**. The examiner can't answer questions about the test, vocabulary or other things, but he/she can repeat.

4 If you can't remember the questions in Part 2 – they are on your **photograph sheet**.

5 Always listen to and answer the question you are asked.

6 Collaborate with your partner in the test. If you don't understand or aren't sure of something in Part 3 and 4, **check** with your partner.

7 Don't dominate your partner in the interactive parts. Part of your mark will be about how well you **interact**.

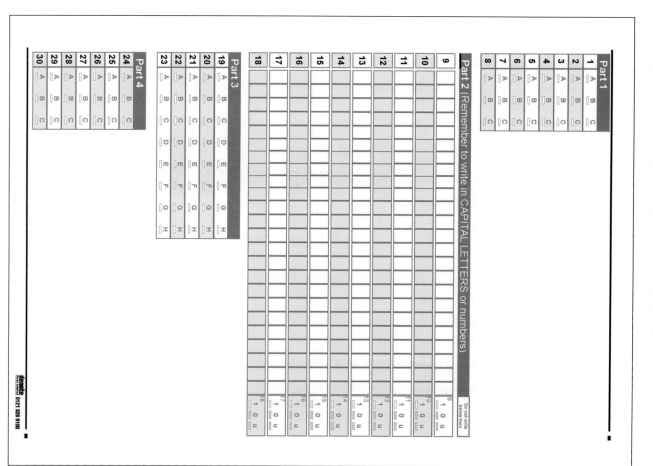

You will hear people talking in eight different situations. For questions 1–8, choose the best answer (A, B or C).

1   You hear two friends talking about a TV drama.

    What was the woman's opinion of it?

    A   It was disappointing.

    B   It was confusing.

    C   It was predictable.

2   You hear a voicemail message.

    Why is the speaker calling?

    A   to cancel an arrangement

    B   to confirm an arrangement

    C   to make a new arrangement

3   You hear a writer talking about her book.

    She admits that she failed to

    A   organise her time well.

    B   have a lot of confidence.

    C   do enough research.

4   You hear two friends talking about a hotel they stayed at.

    What did they both dislike about the hotel?

    A   the location

    B   the room temperature

    C   the time of the morning meal

5   You hear a man talking about a music festival on the radio.

    How does he feel now?

    A   unsurprised by the quantity of litter visitors left

    B   unclear about the logic behind a decision made

    C   disappointed by the amount of money raised

6 You hear a woman talking about preventing the theft of bicycles.

She thinks bike theft has decreased because

A police have been watching affected areas.

B bike racks are constantly being filmed.

C potential thieves have reacted to visual warning.

7 You hear two students talking about a lecture they've been to.

How does the woman feel about it?

A impressed by the amount of information the speaker gave

B inspired to do further research of her own

C relieved that the lecture wasn't too serious

8 You hear two friends talking about a football match.

The woman learns that the match has been

A cancelled because of the condition of the stadium.

B delayed because of the poor weather.

C postponed because of staff shortages.

You will hear a woman called Amy Elliott talking to a group of students about her acting career.

For questions 9–18, complete the sentences with a word or short phrase.

Amy Elliott: My acting career

Amy's (**9**) .... suggested she should try to get a part in the school play.

When she was in a play at (**10**) ...., Amy was spotted for her acting ability.

Amy believes a range of skills such as knowledge of (**11**) .... and costumes are helpful for actors.

One of the characters that Amy has played was inspired by someone she saw on (**12**) ....

Amy's first film role was that of a (**13**) ....

Amy says she hadn't expected to feel so (**14**) .... about going to film in Australia.

On location for her first film, Amy's favourite new sport was (**15**) ....

On Amy's return to the UK, she acted in a (**16**) .... series on TV.

Amy is about to be in a play called (**17**) .... which will tour the UK.

Amy thinks potential actors can gain experience of how a (**18**) .... operates.

Part 3 (CD2: Track 35)

You will hear five short extracts in which people are talking about a course they are doing. For questions 19–23, choose from the list (A–H) what each person appreciates most about the course.

Use the letters only once. There are three extra letters which you do not need to use.

A   the way it leads directly to a particular career

B   the sense of discovery it provides   Speaker 1 [ ] 19

C   the understanding it offers of related subjects   Speaker 2 [ ] 20

D   the way the subject is brought to life   Speaker 3 [ ] 21

E   the academic challenge it provides   Speaker 4 [ ] 22

F   the application of the subject to the real world   Speaker 5 [ ] 23

G   the fact that it helps to build confidence

H   the way it helps to develop a useful life skill

Part 4 (CD2: Track 36)

You will hear part of a radio interview with a culture and technology expert called Andy Davies, who is talking about the use of symbols called 'emojis' in texts and emails. For questions 24–30, choose the best answer (A, B or C).

24 Andy explains that initially, emojis

   A   were simplified versions of the images used today.

   B   were immediately of interest to a certain group of people.

   C   were intended to make international communication easier.

25 What is Andy's opinion about language skills and emoji?

    A   Using emoji too often may have a negative effect on our writing.

    B   Emoji encourage us to exploit a little-used area of the brain.

    C   Making use of emoji enables us to improve our messages.

26 What does Andy like most about how people use emoji?

    A   the imagination used in creating messages

    B   the way statements can be clarified

    C   the personalised application of them

27 How does Andy feel about using emoji himself?

    A   pleased that it strengthens his friendships

    B   annoyed when he can't find a suitable icon

    C   excited about receiving replies to his texts

28 Andy believes that using emojis to express feelings

    A   is something younger people do particularly well.

    B   is more sophisticated than it was in the past.

    C   is a good way to get support from other people.

29 When asked about the possibility of emoji being confusing, Andy says that

    A   it is possible to avoid some misunderstandings.

    B   it is sometimes better to speak to someone in person.

    C   it is irritating when someone misinterprets a text.

30 Andy believes emoji have become so successful because they

    A   are understood on an international scale.

    B   help people stay in touch with each other.

    C   allow people to send messages quickly.

Part 1

Answer these questions.

1 Where are you from?

2 How do you like to spend your free time?

3 What's your best friend like?

4 Have you seen anything interesting on TV recently? What?

5 Are you going to do anything special for your next holiday?

Part 2

Candidate A In this part of the test you are going to have two photographs. You have to talk about your photographs on your own for about a minute, and also answer a question about your partner's photographs.

Candidate A, here are your photographs. They show people in different competitions.

Compare the photographs and say what you think is difficult about taking part in these competitions.

Candidate B, do you enjoy taking part in competitions? Why / Why not?

....

Candidate B Here are your photographs. They show people meeting for different reasons.

Compare the photographs and say why you think the people are meeting.

Candidate A, do you enjoy meeting your friends in cafés? Why / Why not?

Part 3

Now, you have to talk about something together for about two minutes.

Here are some things people can do alone or with others.

Talk about whether it's better to do these things alone or with others.

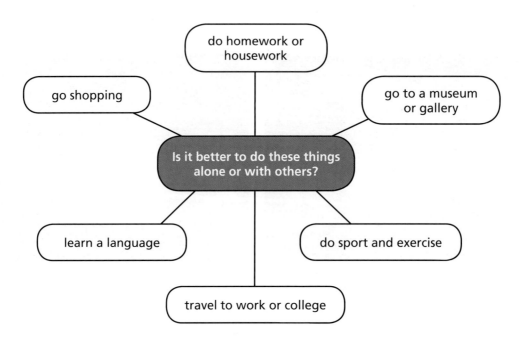

do homework or housework

go shopping

go to a museum or gallery

Is it better to do these things alone or with others?

learn a language

do sport and exercise

travel to work or college

Now you have a minute to decide which of these things is best to do with other people.

Part 4

Answer these questions.

1 Do you think people work together better if they have different skills or similar ones? Why?

2 In your opinion can people be lonely even when they're with a lot of people? Why / Why not?

3 Some people say that it helps to share a problem with someone else. Do you agree? Why / Why not?

4 How important is it to get on well with our classmates or colleagues? Why?

5 Do you think our best friends are the ones with the same interests as us? Why / Why not?

6 Are there any advantages to being an only child?

Unit 1

Listening

Ex 4a and 4b

As a writer, I spend hours parked in front of my laptop, and it's starting to have an impact on my body. I get dry eyes, my neck aches, and I've suffered from repetitive strain injury in my wrist! I should have sorted things out before now – invested in an ergonomic chair which will seat me in the correct position, placed screens at eye level – I just get too carried away to take notice of how I feel physically – it's not until the end of each day that I start to wish I'd stood up and moved around a bit more, or rested my eyes more often.

Ex 5a and 5b

As eye problems in the UK soar among the under 25s, doctors claim that Smartphone addiction is partly to blame – as is the overuse of computers, tablets and flat-screen TVs, many of which emit blue-violet light. Opticians believe this light is potentially dangerous to the back of your eyes. The problem is that users don't blink as often as they should when they're looking at screens, and tend to hold the device closer than when normally looking at objects.

Recent tests show that over-exposure to blue-violet light can increase the chance of developing what's called 'macular degeneration' which is a leading cause of blindness. It can also disrupt our sleep and trigger headaches, amongst other things.

So what's the solution? Getting your eyes tested regularly and having breaks from your computer and phone, say eye-care experts.

Ex 6a and 6b

I reckon Smartphones are making us stupid! They make it harder to learn. I love my Smartphone but everywhere you look, people are glued to their screens – we're missing out on opportunities to appreciate the world around us – that's what really gets to me, people walking about, heads down, staring at screens. It's affecting our ability to focus. I'm not blameless – I can't even watch a film without checking my phone – nothing ever receives my full attention. That's scary, especially in a school context. I'm afraid it affects the quality of my work and how well I learn. And we rely too much on Google instead of our brains.

Ex 7a

Steve, as a doctor, what kind of technology-related injuries do you see amongst teenagers?

Ex 7b

Int. Steve, as a doctor, what kind of technology-related injuries do you see amongst teenagers?

S Well, you'd expect it might be something like sports injuries or sore backs from carrying heavy backpacks to and from school or college. Believe it or not, I see a lot of bumps and scrapes from people who've walked head-long into things when they're texting on the move! The obvious solution is to just stand still while you text. In fact, some governments are introducing a fine for walking and texting at the same time!

EXAM PRACTICE

Ex 1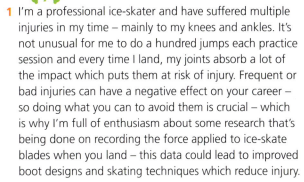

1 I'm a professional ice-skater and have suffered multiple injuries in my time – mainly to my knees and ankles. It's not unusual for me to do a hundred jumps each practice session and every time I land, my joints absorb a lot of the impact which puts them at risk of injury. Frequent or bad injuries can have a negative effect on your career – so doing what you can to avoid them is crucial – which is why I'm full of enthusiasm about some research that's being done on recording the force applied to ice-skate blades when you land – this data could lead to improved boot designs and skating techniques which reduce injury.

2

Int. Gino, tell us about your research into developing better sports helmets.

G Sure. Using sensors placed inside helmets, I've recorded more than 150,000 impacts endured by players. The data helps me understand which situations are most likely to cause head injuries – and how helmets can prevent them. We all know how it hurts when we bang our head, but for most of us that's an occasional thing – not on a daily basis like players, whether they're wearing helmets or not. In my work as a biomedical engineer, I got a call asking which helmets were the best – and discovered that the performance of different brands had never been tested. That's where it all began.

3

M Nice swimsuit!

F Thanks. I thought it was time I invested in some proper gear if I want to make a career of swimming. I guess I had some doubts about the effectiveness of a bit of fabric, but you know what? I reckon I've already shaved a few milliseconds off my race timings.

M Cool! I must admit, I was the same as you at first – and I thought they were pretty ugly as well – but it's been proven that 'technical' swimsuits improve speed and endurance.

F You should get one. There are smart ones for guys!

M It's not on the top of my list for now – and they're pricey.

F But worth every penny!

Speaking

Ex 3

In Part 1 the candidates are asked a few questions and these are all about themselves, about their experiences, their routines, what they enjoy or don't enjoy. There's nothing abstract or complicated here.

We ask individual candidates questions and the candidate replies. We don't ask students to discuss things with their partner at this stage.

This part of the test is important because the candidate can make a good or not so good impression with his or her language.

Candidates need to give answers that not too long or too short! We don't want an answer of about seven words only, but neither do we want long, detailed explanations that go on for a long time and we need to interrupt.

Some candidates prepare their answers to common questions and this is not a good idea, because it doesn't usually sound natural.

One of the reasons for this part of the test is to help candidates relax and stop being nervous. The questions are straightforward and don't require speculation or guesswork.

Ex 4a and 4b

A Yes, I do because I want to be fit.

B Yes, I am doing a few sport every week. I like play football with some of people, they are my friends. We go train on Thursday and sometimes we have match on Saturday.

C Yes, I do. I think it's important to keep fit and I also enjoy competing, so I play tennis matches every weekend at a local club and during the week I often go swimming after work.

D Yes, I really enjoy sport. Every week I go swimming with my friends three or four times. In winter when it's cold I go swimming more often, but during the summer I prefer to spend some time outside and I go walking in the countryside and also I do some riding. We have a stables near us and I get cheap lessons. One day I'd like to have my own horse but they're really expensive to keep. My dad plays a lot of golf and I sometimes go with him …

E I like sports a lot. I started to play tennis when I was five because my parents thought it was good for my health and fitness. It's a nice sport. I have also been in several tennis competitions and I was junior champion at my primary school.

Unit 2

Listening

EXAM PRACTICE 1

Ex 1a and 1b

M I really think I have a great shot of getting into my first choice of university, but I'll apply to a few great backups

… just in case.

F I'm totally getting into my first choice of university – why apply anywhere else?

M What's the point in applying to the university I really want to go to? I doubt I'll make it – it's just a dream.

EXAM PRACTICE 1

Ex 3a (CD1 11)

When I failed my driving test second time around, I just felt like, what's the point – I was so disappointed! But there was no way out of taking it again because I needed a driving licence for the job I wanted. My driving instructor wasn't as sympathetic as I'd expected – she said 'Are you just going to let this defeat you?' I kind of felt annoyed cos it sounded like she was criticising me. Then I realised she was just pushing me to get on with things. It was what I needed to keep going. And guess what? I passed next time round and I'm grateful for what she said now.

EXAM PRACTICE 2

Ex 4 (CD1 12)

S1 I was always telling myself I was useless – I couldn't chat at parties, the words would get stuck in my mouth when I had to speak to more than one or two people... There was some pretty negative talk going on in my head! Then I read this article – it was about making changes to get a more positive outcome. I started asking myself 'What could I do differently?' I know you might be sceptical, but honestly, it's a life-changer and the same could happen to you. Next time I went out, I'd thought of a few things to talk about in case I ran out of conversation!

S2 I remember my first bad basketball match like it was yesterday – I missed five shots in a row in an important tournament. It was embarrassing! Then the club I belonged to got a motivational speaker in – and he said some stuff I've been sharing ever since with anyone who feels bad about their sports performance. It's a bit of psychology really – if you score a fantastic shot, you attribute that to your ability – but if you do something wrong, it just shows you need to practise more.. That way, you're not giving yourself a hard time but just striving to do better. Try it – I haven't had a bad match since!

S3 Every night before I go to bed I write down in my diary three things that went well that day, like someone gave me a compliment or I achieved something at work. It makes you appreciate the good things, I promise! I started doing it after I went through this really awful time last year – my best friend moved away, I broke my wrist, my laptop died and I lost a lot of work. People were telling me to look on the bright side but I was like, are you joking?! Then one of them told me about journal-keeping and now I see stuff that happens much more realistically. You will too.

Speaking
EXAM PRACTICE
Ex 1d CD1 13

Both photographs show people who are feeling really happy because they've done something difficult. They've all got their hands in the air – probably because they're proud of what they've done. In both photographs the men have done something physically hard but the man in the first photograph has been climbing whereas the men in the second have been playing football. The man on the left is alone and there's nobody watching him. The men on the right however are in a team and a big crowd of spectators are watching them. The photographs were taken in very different places too. The climber is in a beautiful outdoor location – in the mountains - while the footballers are in a stadium. In both photographs the men are wearing clothes that help them do their sport or activity easily. The climber has probably chosen his own clothes, but the football team have been told what to wear! I think the main difference between the photographs is that the footballers are taking part in an organised sport whereas the climber climbs whenever and wherever he wants to.

Unit 3

Listening
Ex 2b and 4 CD1 14

1 Today I'm going to talk about CCTV and how good an idea it is – or isn't. Opinion on the subject is of course divided, so I aim to present both sides of the argument.

Some people say that CCTV invades our privacy when we're out in public, whereas others think that if you've done nothing wrong, there is no need to worry about being filmed in public.

Let's look at the arguments presented by those in favour of CCTV first of all …

2

M How far have you got with the essay on the right to privacy?

F Erm, well, I've started my introduction and kind of sketched out a plan for the rest of it.

M Ah, right. Don't they say you should leave the intro til last?

F Well, you don't have to – I wanted to just present the opposing points of view first, decide what it is I'm going to discuss – then I'll revise it at the end I guess.

3

Int. Dan, you run a CCTV firm. Do you ever consider the implications of what you're doing?

D You mean, do I think about whether CCTV is right or wrong? Sure I do. Obviously, I fall down on the side of it being a positive thing – you know, cameras act as deterrents – they might put someone off committing a crime if they know they're being watched. And the

footage is useful for the police – they're able to solve crimes more quickly by being able to identify criminals.

Int. Mm, but what about the other side of the coin? I mean …

4 The police have reported a fifty per cent or more drop in the number of crimes being solved using CCTV footage in the last five years, claiming that the poor quality of the images is what makes it challenging to correctly identify those who have committed criminal acts. The effect of CCTV on reducing crime has always been considered a strong argument in support of having cameras in public places, and this news comes as a disappointment to organisations whose objective is to make our streets safer. Here with us to discuss the issue is Chief Constable …

Ex 3a, 3b and 4 CD1 15

5

F Did you read that article about the 'Big Brother' phenomenon?

M You mean about us being watched? CCTV and all that? Yeah, it was interesting. I thought it was a bit one-sided though.

F It did go on about the positives a bit more than the negatives, I agree. It was kind of making a lot of the whole crime prevention thing, wasn't it?

M Yeah – they didn't really say too much about the invasion of privacy, did they?

6

Int. So, who's going to start the debate today? Jenny, you're on the 'anti' team for CCTV. Would you like to start us off?

J Yep! I think that having CCTV in public places is an attack on our freedom. Why? Because the government and private companies shouldn't be given the opportunity to record what we do. Most governments and companies do nothing with the CCTV footage they collect. But what if it falls into the wrong hands?

Int. Thanks, Jenny. Who'd like to counteract Jenny's argument? Arran, have you got an argument in favour?

7

M I reckon if people want to commit a crime, they're going to go ahead and do it whether they're being filmed or not. I mean, you can just disguise yourself, can't you? Wear a hoodie or mask or whatever so their faces can't be seen – you see that all the time on TV.

F Yeah, and actually CCTV cameras aren't even intended to stop serious crimes, but to make money! Think about those cameras on the roads that film you driving along in a bus lane – you might only be getting out of the way of an obstruction but then you go and get fined cos you weren't supposed to be there.

8 So, as a conclusion to our crime prevention week, I'd like to give you this week's English assignment. I'd like you to discuss this statement in response to the usage of CCTV cameras: 'If you have nothing to hide, you have nothing to worry about'. I'd like you to prepare a short presentation to give in class next week, offering your opinions about the value of CCTV to society. You could think about our right to privacy, or you might like to consider the safety aspect of having cameras in city centres.

EXAM PRACTICE

Ex 2b

1 Although many people might assume drones to be a new thing – they're seen on news reports and in the skies – they've actually been in existence for a considerable amount of time – right back to the First World War in fact, when basic remote-controlled aircraft were used. So, the idea of having a pilotless aircraft is far from a new one. Today there are multiple types of drone performing different functions. The most sophisticated of these can fly very high – up to 20,000 metres – and the fastest can travel at an unbelievable 21,000 kilometres per hour. That means a drone can fly from London, England, to Sydney, Australia in less than an hour!

2 As you may or may not know, drones are used for many things. As well as the military, who've used them for some time, drones have many other uses – delivering medical supplies or helping farmers keep an eye on their crops. They've even been used by the paparazzi to take photos of celebrities. Imagine looking up while you're in the garden and seeing a drone flying over! I can't say I'm comfortable with this particular usage, though no one can deny the usefulness of drones for certain situations where it might be difficult to fly into – remote areas or war zones, where drones can drop urgent supplies such as food and water.

3

F Wow! I never realised drones were used for anything other than military stuff, did you?

M Well, yeah, we did this thing about them last year at my school.

F Don't you think it's a bit like spying? I mean, what about privacy? We're already under huge amounts of surveillance – CCTV cameras on every street corner. Drones could invade our private space too!

M I dunno if I'm with you there – I mean, who'd be interested in spying on me? I don't do anything particularly interesting!

F I still think they're seen pretty negatively, don't you? And they're becoming more affordable – so anyone could get one and put it to the wrong use.

4

F What do you think the future of drones is?

M I'm confident that they're going to play an important part in our everyday routines before too long. The Amazon website has already started testing unmanned drones

to deliver packages – so in the next couple of years, you could have your books and music left on your doorstep by a drone! You might not like the sound of not having human contact but it's very possible. And think of all the other ways they could be used – already pizza deliveries are taking place by drones – the possibilities are endless if you think about it, especially as they're becoming smaller and more efficient.

Speaking

Ex 3b and 3c

A OK, so we have to think about how important it is to have rules about these things. Shall we start with this one – throwing rubbish in the streets?

B Yes, good place to start! I think it's really important because otherwise the streets get dirty and untidy. In my town you get a fine if you litter the streets and our streets are very, very clean. What do you think?

A I completely agree. I would hope that people wouldn't need rules for this, but some people do because they just don't care. They think about themselves and can't be bothered to put their rubbish in a bin! How about this one – using mobiles in theatres? I think it's incredible that people do this – and you know, they also film live performances on their phones. They should be thrown out of the theatre! How do you feel about it?

B Too right they should! It must be horrible for the actors – all they see is little red lights in the audience - very off putting. Now, this one about making a lot of noise is interesting. Should there be rules about it? What's your view?

A In fact, I think it's really important. If groups of kids are making a lot of noise in the streets late at night it isn't a good thing for the people who live there. Or if you've got a neighbour who plays loud music all the time – it must be hard. Don't you agree?

B Well, I partly agree with you! If people make a lot of noise regularly, then yes – there should be rules about it. But if it's just a one-off – you know, like a twenty first birthday party or something, then no, definitely not.

A I still think they need to consider the people who live near them. OK, let's move on to smoking. Ah – I think you and I are going to have different views here! In our country you can't smoke in a public place, like restaurants, shops and they are trying to make rules about smoking in parks and squares too …

Interlocutor Thank you.

Unit 4

Listening

Ex 2a

There's no doubt about it.

No way!

Tell me about it!

I'm not sure I'm with you there.

We'll have to agree to disagree.

You've got a point.

I don't know about that.

Absolutely!

I couldn't agree more.

That's not necessarily the case.

I guess so.

I don't think so.

Ex 3b and 4b

M Volunteering's a really valuable thing to do in my opinion. I mean, you can really make a difference to other people's lives.

F That's for sure! Did I tell you about my gap year? When I helped out on a volunteering project?

M No – what did you do?

F Oh, I went to this elephant sanctuary abroad, where they look after elephants so they aren't used for labour.

M Aww, that must have been so worthwhile!

F Totally! The elephants seem so happy and well-fed, and they live longer and more healthily. It's so sweet to watch them playing in the water! I just helped out with cleaning and stuff – sounds hard work, I know.

M You must have got a lot out of the experience!

F Yeah, I did. I didn't mind the dirty work! Have you ever done any volunteering?

M Not yet, but I'd like to.

Ex 5a and 5b

F What do you reckon about those people who do, like, a hundred marathons in a year or something silly like that – in order to raise money for charity?

M Erm, I don't know, really. I mean, are they doing it for themselves so they look good or genuinely doing it to help other people?

F What does it matter? I suppose if someone's benefitting through someone else giving up their time to help out or take part in challenges or even just make a donation – I can't see the problem in that.

M Sure – though I bet most people wouldn't do something they really hated for the sake of others.

F Probably not!

Ex 7

F Did you read that article about helping others?

M Oh, yeah! Some of the anecdotes in it were fascinating…

F I know – there was one which made me go awwww! The one where a woman bought a burger for a homeless guy and he said he was vegetarian and couldn't eat it?

M Oh, yeah – especially when I got to the bit about how she asked him what he liked eating and then went back with some noodles for him! So lovely of her.

F Mm, and then after that she set went round to all the homeless kitchens in the city – where people go and get a hot meal once a day – and made sure they all included a couple of vegetarian options on their menus.

M She made a real difference, didn't she?

F Mm. It's easy to pass by people on the street who need help if you're in a rush isn't it?

M You mean leave someone else to do it? I feel too guilty to walk on by!

F But, say in the case of homeless people, for example – I feel helpless if I don't have any change in my purse to give them. It's hard to meet their eye – I feel ashamed.

M Well, it's a matter of opinion I guess. You can always go back with something later – and let them know you're going to.

EXAM PRACTICE

Ex 1

1

F Have you ever done any random acts of kindness – you know, where you're just going about your business and see someone needs a hand and you help them?

M Of course! It doesn't cost much to help someone out, does it – you know, like how much effort is it to pick up something someone's dropped or something?

F Not much, I guess! I ought to take a leaf out of your book.

M What do you mean?

F Well, I usually just let someone else deal with it cos it seems inconvenient, but it isn't really.

M A lot of people do the same as you – don't feel bad about it!

F Maybe I should!

2

F I've always been too shy to speak up about things, even if I want them to be different.

M Like what?

F Well, some people at work always grab the best holiday dates for themselves and some people end up having to take their holidays at less convenient times. There should be a rota system, so people take turns for their first choice of dates.

M What's so hard about suggesting that?

F I don't like to make a fuss about things in the office.

M You could go directly to your boss – your colleagues wouldn't need to know.

F Mm… It's ok for you – you're confident! I don't want to be seen as a trouble-maker!

M You wouldn't!

3

M I need to get in better shape.

F I know what you mean – talking about myself of course! I can't jog around the block without getting out of breath!

M It isn't as though we stuff ourselves full of chips and chocolate, though, is it?

F True. And I'm always careful to avoid snacks before bedtime.

M Mm, it can interrupt your sleep while you're digesting – and some things give you nightmares or keep you awake.

F I can do without that – I really need my sleep! Anyway, what are we going to do?

M Let's make a plan of action. We could start small and do something every day til we feel better.

F Cool.

Speaking

Ex 4a and 4c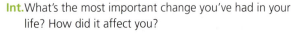

Int. What's the most important change you've had in your life? How did it affect you?

Cand. OK - The most important change in my life. Well, that's got to be when my parents moved to France to live because of my dad's job. I was about eleven and at first it was awful. The worst thing was that I had to leave all my friends behind. At that time social media wasn't that big so it was hard to keep in touch. But, I met loads of new friends, obviously and one big benefit was that I got really good at French!

Ex 4b and 4c

Int. Are there any aspects of your lifestyle that you would like to change? Why?

Cand. A Oh yes. For example – I'm not very sporty and I don't get a lot of exercise, so I think that's one change I need to make. I ought to do more sporty things like going to the gym or for a swim. But I think I'm just too lazy. For instance, if a friend phones me up and suggests going for a run – I'd much rather stay in front of the TV. I've got into some bad habits – such as using my car to go everywhere instead of walking! Terrible I know!

Cand. B Can I say something here? I'd like to add that I think a lot of people are the same as Paulo. I'm definitely like him. I think we work so hard and there are so many interesting things to do at home – watch good TV, films, go online, play computer games … that we're tempted NOT to do much exercise!

Unit 5

Listening

Ex 2a and 2b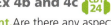

If you met Ed Sheeran in the street, you probably wouldn't know he was a pop star! With his messy, uncombed hair and crumpled clothes that haven't seen an iron in a while, Ed looks more like the boy next door than a millionaire. But he is now one of the world's most successful singer-songwriters, with a best-selling album in over 65 countries.

Ex 3a and 3b

Ed Sheeran's my number one singer song-writer. I love his stuff. He started writing songs when he was only thirteen – imagine! He can play loads of instruments – guitar, bass, drums, cello, piano! I reckon Ed totally deserves the respect he's gained from famous songwriters as well – and he's still so young. I was reading this interview with Ed and he said that Paul McCartney – you know, one of the singers from The Beatles – came over to him after a gig he did at the closing ceremony of the Olympics in London, and he said he liked Ed's music. Ed was like, blown away! I would've been too!

Ex 4a

M Do you follow Ed Sheeran on Twitter?

F No, but I like his music. Why?

M Well, he posted this thing about how he was giving his whole wardrobe to a bunch of charity shops – and the charities raised more than £6,000 by auctioning Ed's old sweatshirts on eBay!

F That's cool! I also heard that he's a clean-freak – you wouldn't think so cos he looks a bit scruffy, but apparently he showers twice a day cos he likes to smell nice!

M Hm, you wouldn't think that from his appearance, would you? He seems like a really cool guy, though, doesn't he?

F Yeah, really down to earth – not like some musicians you hear about!

EXAM PRACTICE

Ex 1

1

M What do you think of Rafaella? I like her music, but she's a bit of a diva by the sounds of it.

F I know – I heard she refuses to meet fans personally and she'll only have her photo taken from a certain angle. How arrogant!

M Really? I wonder what gives these musicians such huge egos? Do you think the fame goes to their head?

F It must do – all those people screaming and wanting your autograph. It must be hard to stay level-headed with that going on – people thinking you're the best thing since sliced bread!

M Well, some celebrities seem to manage to keep their feet on the ground and stay normal!

2

M Many singers and actors can become difficult to work with because of their demanding behaviour as they lose touch with reality. Mariah Carey likes her dressing room to be filled with white doves; Beyoncé insists on rose-scented candles and spicy chicken. So how and why does a celebrity change from grounded girl-next-door to a demanding diva? A study on fame indicates that as a celebrity becomes more famous, their relationship with the world changes. In a world where a celebrity is hardly ever told 'no', a self-centred orientation can occur. It's easy to lose perspective when you're surrounded by an army of adoring fans and publicists who will do anything to please.

3

F I think the deal is not to buy into the whole 'I'm better than everyone else cos I'm famous' thing. I don't take myself too seriously. It's important not to get out of touch with what's really going on, not to become a prima donna. I consider myself a laidback kind of person, easy-going. Acting isn't important! I'm not saving anybody's life – I'm just making movies. I've seen celebrities talk down to those around them, start demanding all kinds of ridiculous things in their dressing rooms – I don't get it, no matter how famous they are. They need to get over themselves, stop becoming full of themselves – they're just doing a job!

Speaking

Ex 3a

Milton, it's your turn first. Here are your photographs. They show people listening to music in different places. I'd like you to compare the photographs and say why you think the people have chosen to listen to music in these places.

Ex 3b and 3c

As you say, both photographs show people listening to music but they are in different places. The first picture shows a lot of people at a music festival. It's a really big event and some people are sitting a long way from the stage, whereas the second picture shows a couple listening to someone who is playing music in the street. They are very close to the performer and can hear the music very clearly and well. The festival goers, on the other hand certainly can't see the performers very clearly and might not hear them very well either! I prefer the first picture because I like music festivals and I go quite often. They're great fun. It looks cold but that doesn't matter. I'd like to be there!

Unit 6

Listening

Ex 2a and 2b

How do you find water in the driest deserts? Or explore the ocean's depths? Questions like these puzzled the world's smartest engineers for a long time. But whatever they came up with was no match for Mother Nature … Millions of years of evolution have created organisms with amazing abilities. Realising this, engineers have set to work borrowing from nature's most brilliant adaptations to answer their problems and invent processes and products to solve problems. This is known as biomimicry, and it's used in a wide range of fields – energy, architecture, medicine, agriculture … For instance, dolphins have taught us how to send signals under water and we've learned how to create sustainable buildings from insects.

Ex 5 and 7

This is my idea for the biomimicry competition! It's such a fascinating thing to be involved in – not that I'm saying it wasn't hard work – there was a ton of reading to do. Once I'd done a bit of research, though, I knew what I wanted to focus on. I'm a fridge magnet collector – wherever I go I pick one up. But some of them aren't that great for actually holding onto things – like my to-do lists! – they slip down the fridge door – annoying! So, I've invented a kind of suction thing – based on the sticky feet of insects. Isn't it amazing how they 'sit' on the ceiling?

EXAM PRACTICE

Ex 1a

1

M I read this article about a robot crab last night.

F Yeah! It's cool, huh? I've always been fascinated by the world under the sea.

M It was interesting to see how it operates – it's like a massive creature walking over the seabed surveying for oil spills and other stuff. As for what lives down there – that's not my thing really.

F It can do what divers can't – they get swept around by the strong currents. Much as I'm interested in marine life, I wouldn't be too keen on being in the depths of the sea myself.

M I did go diving once actually – my brother made me go with him.

F Wow!

2

F Robotic fish looks and moves like a real fish – but don't be fooled! It patrols the seas for pollution – say someone's dumping chemicals or there's a leak. It took a while to get this off the ground – a lot of hard work's gone into it. Of course, it can be a real challenge getting the right amount of money to move a project forward – in the case of Robotic fish, it's been pretty straightforward – its usefulness is clear to everyone involved. It makes a change for me, as most of the projects I've been on have been low-budget so far. I'm still stunned by how quickly the whole thing took off!

3

M As you know, there are parts of the world where water's scarce – so finding better ways to gather water is a major concern. It's vital that scientists look to nature for solutions – which is where the Namib Desert beetle comes in. This amazing insect gets all the water it needs by catching ocean fog that rolls over the desert. Its back is rough and covered in ridges, and when enough water collects on it, the drops roll into the beetle's mouth. Fog nets are already used to collect water – but new developments in textured surfaces inspired by the beetle could help researchers revolutionise the way water is collected – about time too!

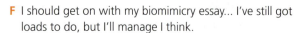

4

F I should get on with my biomimicry essay... I've still got loads to do, but I'll manage I think.

M Yeah. I'm doing the snakebot – it can cross deserts just like snakes do.

F Ah, yeah – they've invented it one that can move across sand right? Actually, I can't see the point of that.

M Oh, it's gonna be useful. Like, one day they reckon it'll be able to squeeze into collapsed buildings to find anyone trapped there – or explore pyramids, stuff like that.

F Oh, OK. It took me a while to decide what to do – I didn't want our teacher saying it was the wrong kind of thing.

M You'll be fine.

Speaking

Ex 3a and 3b

A In the second picture there's a farmer I think with his sheep and a dog... it's a special **type** of dog that farmers use to make the sheep go in a particular direction. Sorry, I don't know the name **in** English.

B If the sheep are in different places in the field, it's the dog's job to ... oh, what's the **word** ... it's **when** it runs round them and brings them all together.

C The farmer often has a ... it's a **thingummy** ... something he puts in his mouth to give signals to the dog. Sorry, I can't remember the **exact** word.

D In the picture there's a woman with quite a big dog. It's a ... oh, what do you **call** that dog, it's the dog that leads people when they can't see, when they're blind.

E The woman is holding the dog on a ... Oh, I used to know the word **for** this ... it's the **same** thing that people put round them when they go rock climbing and things like that.

F The woman is also holding a ... oh, **what** is it ... it's got fire at the end, sorry ... it's **gone**.

Unit 7

Listening

Ex 2b

Consumerism has two dictionary definitions. The first defines it as the state of an advanced industrial society in which a lot of goods are bought and sold. The second defines it as the situation in which too much attention is given to buying and owning things.

Ex 3b

a I go online every day looking at new clothes and I go shopping every weekend.

b I might buy something new if I'm going to an event or party.

c I find out what's 'in' by checking previews on my favourite brands' Facebook pages.

d I read all the fashion magazines every week to find out what's currently 'on trend'.

e I look in shop windows when I'm passing.

f I'm not very passionate about shopping – my five-year-old trainers are fine!

EXAM PRACTICE

Ex 1a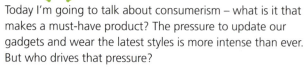

Today I'm going to talk about consumerism – what is it that makes a must-have product? The pressure to update our gadgets and wear the latest styles is more intense than ever. But who drives that pressure?

Let me give you an example of what I'm talking about. At the launch of the latest iPhone, more than a thousand people queued outside the Apple store in London's Covent Garden in the UK. Consumers arrived from as far away as Norway, just to get the gadget. They just *had* to have it. But why?

Well, thanks to sophisticated manufacturing, companies can make small changes to the design of popular items easily and quickly. Changes to the colour or shape of a product can make it look completely new. As a result, must-have items that are only a few months old may already begin to look dated very quickly – which is what drives consumers to update their existing product as soon as they can. In reality, the phone, for example, may be very similar to what someone's already got, but might be in a different colour. But still consumers *really* want it!

Another reason for constantly changing and updating our gadgets is something called 'planned obsolescence'. Some manufacturers plan for their products to work less well after a certain amount of time, which pushes consumers to buy new models. It can affect electronics, such as laptops, tablets, mobile phones and printers that require software updates. Studies have shown that every time technology giants, such as Apple launch a new phone, there is an increase in complaints about older versions running more slowly! There's a lot of psychology going on, isn't there?

And let's not forget the power of the media on consumers' attitudes. Celebrities can have a very powerful effect on brands, and their endorsement can make the shoe or the Smartphone appear to be more glamorous and cool. By buying that same product, we hope a little bit of the cool will rub off on us! When cool brands like Nike and Adidas produce new trainers, for example, which are then seen on the feet of the famous – no matter what field they're in, be it sports or music – they instantly become the in thing with young consumers. Whoever they are and whatever they're famous for – I guess if we want to identify with them, they will naturally have a direct influence on what we buy.

Of course, there's nothing like a bit of peer pressure to get us wanting more! People have always like to copy one another, but the increased use of social media makes us compare ourselves to a bigger circle of friends. You see three of your friends wearing the latest brands in their Instagram or Facebook pictures in the same week, and suddenly, the urge to get the item for yourself is overwhelming – even if you hadn't noticed the brand before.

Speaking

Ex 5b

Both pictures show people out shopping. There are two couples – both girls. They look quite young, maybe late teens or early twenties and it looks as if they're quite close friends because they're helping each other to choose different things. In the first photograph the girls are obviously shopping for clothes. However it isn't that clear in the second photograph. They could be shopping for anything really because they're looking in a shop window and we can't see what they're looking at. In each picture one of the girls is using a phone to take a picture. In the first photo I guess she's taking it to show the other girl what the dress looks like or maybe to send to another friend for advice. In the second picture the girl could well be checking some information online. I would say that she's comparing prices of things before she buys something. There's another possibility. She might be photographing something in the window to look at later and to compare with other photos she takes of things on this shopping trip.

Unit 8

Listening

Ex 8b

1 People sometimes say there's a 'glass ceiling' in certain professions – a barrier to career advancement for women and minorities.

2 My cousin is a professional snowboarder – he gets paid to take part in competitions.

3 It is simply not acceptable to discriminate against people of a particular race or gender in the workplace.

4 I'm thinking of setting up my own business making jewellery from broken glass.

5 I haven't been granted permission for all the leave I've requested this year.

6 My children have no ambition whatsoever!

EXAM PRACTICE

Ex 2

Hi, I'm Sabrina Carlotti, and I'm here to talk to you about what it takes to become a travel writer.

People often ask me what my job is – they think I'm just going off on yet another foreign holiday, but nothing could be further from the truth. Sometimes I travel all over the globe researching stories for the magazine I write for, but I also spend a considerable amount of time with my colleagues in the editorial department in San Francisco, making sure every page of the magazine keeps readers engaged.

I'm not always writing about exotic locations either! Sometimes my job involves writing about a place people have been to a hundred times and giving them the inspiration to see it in a fresh way. That means a lot of exploring locally and trying new things – even in your own backyard, and although you might not be all that keen to do it – I'm terrified of

heights, yet for the sake of my job I've abseiled down a building and done a bungee jump – it might be what the job entails. You might even get involved in local environmental projects, for example, which need a bit of promotion further afield.

Another question I often get asked is how come I ended up doing this. Well, I was lucky enough to have parents who could afford to take me and my sister away during school holidays and we had some unforgettable trips. These were often to some mind-blowing locations, but the times we camped out for the night in the back garden, or explored the local woods at the end of the street got me just as excited.

When I got older, the desire to explore the world got even stronger. I travelled whenever I could – even when I had little money as a student I'd go and work on an organic farm in the south of France, or be an au pair for the summer in Switzerland. I didn't get that much time off, but when I did, I'd be straight on the bus and whizzing off to see the local sights. Not all of them were glamorous, but a tiny village off the beaten track was just as incredible to me as a major city. Then when I was at college I chose to go and live in Germany to complete my studies. All these experiences gave me a lot to talk about when interviewing for travel-writing jobs. I also took a publishing course through the Columbia University journalism school one summer, which helped introduce me to the industry and I came away with some valuable contacts.

I get paid to do what I love, and I travel all over to meet people, eat food, and see sights that I never would have heard of otherwise. I don't get to choose where I go to next, but I can put in a request if I know they need to send someone to a country I've never been to, or desperately want to go back to.

If you're interested in becoming a travel writer you can figure out the basics of editing a magazine or website on the job. What no one can do is teach you to have passion or become an expert in the field. If it's something you think you might be good at, keep reading about what you love, and maybe even start a blog to fine-tune your talents. Don't worry if you can't get overseas – writing about your local area with conviction will convince potential employers of your confidence and what you're worth to their team.

One thing to bear in mind is that every field is becoming more technical than ever. You're highly unlikely as a writer to need to know how to code, but computer and social media skills are key. Make yourself attractive by becoming an expert on basic computer programs, and work on building a professional online presence – and don't be embarrassed to shout about your achievements to those who might be able to offer you a job!

Speaking

Ex 3b

A First, a good salary, that's very important.

B You're right, it is. What about a modern work place? That's when they have fun office areas and things like ping pong breaks for the staff I think.

A Yes, and where you can wear what you like to work, not suits and stuff. Mmm. It's important, isn't it?

B Yes. I think it isn't important to have friendly colleagues. What do you think?

A No, it's nice. But it isn't always possible. It's more important that you have interesting work.

B Yes, I agree. And it's good too if you can get promotion.

A Yes. That's very important.

Ex 3d (CD2 9)

A It isn't always possible to be happy at work but it helps if you are, doesn't it?

B Oh yes – we spend a lot of our lives at work. What about a good salary? How important is that do you think?

A It depends what you mean by a good salary. I don't think it needs to be very high for people to be happy - as long as it is enough for people to have a basically good standard of living.

B I totally agree. I mean, you need to live and eat and not have to worry too much about money, but for me that would be enough. Then we've got a modern work place. I imagine that refers to the facilities and attitude of the employers to helping staff to relax and do things like play table football in their breaks.

A I think you're right. Again – I would say that it would be good to have those things, but it's not vital for a happy working life.

B Here I have to disagree! I think it makes a lot of difference if you can relax and have fun at work. Otherwise you might get bored or too stressed out to do your job.

A OK, you've got a point there! Now, work colleagues. For me it's essential to have friendly people round you when you work. They can help make your life easier and make the time you spend at work more enjoyable.

B Very true!

Unit 9

Listening
Ex 2 (CD2 10)

The day's just started and already you've got that awful feeling in your stomach at the thought of all that stuff you have to do – the chores are piling up at home, you need to catch up with friends you haven't seen for ages, and there are a million emails to answer! Oh – and you've got to finish that report for this afternoon. Help! Yes, you could go into avoidance mode and mess about on Twitter while your to-do list increases by the minute. Or you could learn the art of time management. Today we'll be talking to …

Ex 3 (CD2 11)

S1 I work from home and I *do* get all my work done – it's just that it probably takes twice as long as it should! It's hard to find a balance between what sometimes feels like torture – you know, getting that really tedious task done – and fun. Sometimes I find I reward myself for doing even the tiniest task – making myself a sandwich, watching catch-up TV, when really I ought to be getting on with the next part of what I've got to do.

S2 I've got admit that I do find it hard to find the time for everything I've got to fit in – like a full-time job, getting to football practice three nights a week, studying for a course I'm doing for work in the evenings, keeping my flat clean and tidy, and then fitting in time to see my girlfriend! I need help finding time for relaxation – I'm way too focussed all the time and need to chill out a bit more!

S3 I have a pretty full social calendar but I'm known as the one who's always late – usually cos I've set off in the wrong direction thinking I'm on the way to some other event that was last month or later this week or whatever! Either that or I can't find my car keys or it took longer than I thought to iron my clothes, have a shower and so on! I don't know what I'm supposed to be doing when. That makes me stressed and even more behind.

Ex 4a (CD2 12)

S1 When people have a to-do list as long as their arm, most of them do the easy stuff first. But leaving the more challenging things til last sets up an 'avoid it' goal rather than a 'do it' one. If you tackle the task you dread most right away, there'll be no need to procrastinate any more!

S2 If you're overwhelmed with things to do, you may need to drop some commitments – but you shouldn't see that as a negative or a failure. Just think about what your goals in life are and stick with things which will help you achieve them. Lose the things that stress you out, like those piano lessons you never practise for.

S3 A killer to-do list is vital to success. Trying to keep everything in your head without making a note of it creates mental clutter – which results in extreme forgetfulness. Fortunately, there are a ton of to-do list apps out there – but it can also be fun to do it the old-fashioned way and keep a notebook – it's really satisfying to physically cross stuff off a list!

EXAM PRACTICE
Ex 2a and 2c (CD2 13)

S1 I used to be a procrastinator. I'd spend so long trying to decide what to do that it would be too late to do anything by the time I'd reached a conclusion! And I'd be so easily distracted – I'd start making shopping lists in the middle of the morning at my desk, or catch up on the news instead of doing the cleaning. I know experts say get the tough stuff out of the way so you can relax – and it's a great idea in principal. What works for me now, is finding little slots in the day where I can squeeze stuff in – like reading emails on the bus to work.

S2 I used to rush about from one thing to another, and sometimes didn't even have time to eat proper meals. I used to wish there were more hours in the day! In the end I had to give myself a good talking to – my health was suffering. I set aside a bit of time each evening to think about the following day – this means I know what I'm meant to be doing when. Of course, sometimes it all goes out of the window when something unexpected happens. I just keep the day's tasks in my head – though I know some people prefer to use a diary to make a note of stuff.

S3 I do this thing called 'SPIFY' – short periods of intense focus. Basically, I work really hard with all my concentration for 45 minutes before taking 15 minutes out every hour. I think some people would disagree with the thought of that but it's very effective. I do more work in a day now than I ever did before – I'd sit and waste time on meaningless tasks rather than getting on with it. I've passed the SPIFY idea on to my team and now we're getting through our workload more efficiently and we're much less stressed! I feel like I'm in control of time now, instead of the other way round!

S4 I never really kept a to-do list and consequently found I was always overlooking things I had to do and being constantly late on deadlines. I was always on the go – I could never say no to anything and ended up feeling pretty stressed out. So, I decided to give it a go and it's made such a difference! It's so satisfying putting a line through things as they're completed. I use some software on the computer – not a diary as such, but I can set it to give me reminders and it works brilliantly. Now I never miss a deadline or appointment and I feel a lot more relaxed.

S5 At one point I was trying to fit so much in I'd try and do two tasks at once – cleaning my teeth while I loaded the washing machine and stuff like that. I never had a minute to myself. And when I did get a short break from my hectic schedule I didn't know what to do! Then I saw a programme about time management and something called 'streamlining your choices' – looking for areas where you can save time. For example, I'd spend ages putting outfits together for work – now I've got a bunch of colour-coordinated clothes – whatever I pull out of the drawer goes with everything else. I've got at least an hour a week back!

Speaking
Ex 5a and 5b

Int. Thank you. Now you have about a minute to decide which of these things people should spend most time doing.

A OK. So, which of these should we spend MOST time doing? What do you think?

B That's tricky. I guess it depends on each person. I suppose if it's getting close to exams then students should spend most of their free time on preparing. Do you agree?

A mmm, not really! I mean, yes – that's important, but even when you've got exams, you still need to chill out – like watch some TV or listen to some music.

B Yeah, I see your point. Sometimes we obsess too much about work and then our brains get tired.

A And even when people have a job, they often spend too much time thinking about work. It isn't the most important thing, is it?

B No, it isn't! Some people might want to spend a lot of time relaxing on their own. I think my dad would! But for me the most important thing is contacting friends. It's really important to chat to people or email them and share your news and stuff.

B Yes, and as we said everyone should do regular exercise but it needn't take loads of time. Just ten minutes can be good for you.

A I completely agree with you. But, although I think contacting friends should take up a lot of time, I think we should spend more time on actually having fun – like going out to the cinema, parties...even shopping with mates! Life's too short to spend it all working or online.

B That is very true! I think you've persuaded me! Let's go for 'having fun.'

Unit 10

Listening
Ex 3c (CD2 15)

Minecraft is a simple video game that's become one of the most addictive and best selling in the world, having gained tens of millions of players around the globe since it was released in 2011. It's about breaking and placing blocks, and has two separate game modes – Creative and Survival. The former attracts players fascinated by the opportunity to construct buildings of any shape or size – there's nothing to fight against, and unlimited access to building materials. The latter draws in those who love a bit of adventure – in the Survival mode, you build out of necessity, protecting yourself against baddies keen to destroy your world. The game can be played on any device – from a PlayStation or Xbox to a PC or Mac, to an Android or Apple Smartphone. So it's easy to play whether you're at home or on the move!

Ex 4c (CD2 16)
Answer 1

Mm, that's an interesting question. Anything which gets young people thinking and making decisions for themselves has to be beneficial, right? It's the same stuff that teachers help them develop in school or at university. Gaming keeps the brain active, flexible – develops independence of mind – in the same way that solving maths problems, discussing ideas, or writing poetry might.

Answer 2

Well, you might think it's perfectly understandable that parents are bothered about addiction and eyesight and things like that… but far from being a mindless activity requiring little brainpower, a lot of games, such as Minecraft, actually improve skills. It's a shame parents overlook things like the creativity, teamwork, and problem-solving that gaming develops – all the same stuff kids learn when they're involved in outdoor activities, which is still the preference of many parents.

Answer 3

Minecraft's based on a pretty simple idea – building with cubes of various materials such as sand, volcanic lava or rock – which the player chooses themselves. Let's focus on the Survival mode for a minute. Surviving the game's all down to your ability to construct shelters from whatever materials you've selected and make items to kill off the games' monsters! I guess destroying the enemy has universal appeal, doesn't it? The community of people involved with the game numbers tens of millions.

EXAM PRACTICE

Ex 1a and 1b

F What do you think is the reason for the popularity of the video game Minecraft?

M Minecraft's based on a pretty simple idea – building with cubes of various materials such as sand, volcanic lava or rock – which the player chooses themselves. Let's focus on the Survival mode for a minute. Surviving the game's all down to your ability to construct shelters from whatever materials you've selected and make items to kill off the games' monsters! I guess destroying the enemy has universal appeal, doesn't it? The community of people involved with the game numbers tens of millions.

F Many parents think playing video games is bad for their kids. What do you think about this?

M Well, you might think it's perfectly understandable that parents are bothered about addiction and eyesight and things like that… but far from being a mindless activity requiring little brainpower, a lot of games, such as Minecraft, actually improve skills. It's a shame parents overlook things like the creativity, teamwork, and problem-solving that gaming develops – all the same stuff kids learn when they're involved in outdoor activities, which is still the preference of many parents.

F So, would you say Minecraft is educational?

M Mm, that's an interesting question. Anything which gets young people thinking and making decisions for themselves has to be beneficial, right? It's the same stuff that teachers help them develop in school or at university. Gaming keeps the brain active, flexible – develops independence of mind – in the same way that solving maths problems, discussing ideas, or writing poetry might.

Speaking

Ex 3a and 3b

Candidate A

In both photographs people are playing computer games competitively. They are in different places. They are competing for different reasons. In the first picture it's a big competition. It's in a big room. There are lots of people playing at the same time. In the second picture there are two people playing. They are at home in a living room. I think they're friends. It's probably a friendly game. The winner is not important. In the first picture they all want to win the competition.

Candidate B

The people in the first picture are playing computer games in a big competition. There are lots of people in the competition and they are in a big room. They are wearing headphones and I'm not sure why. Perhaps they need to hear music or instructions. Maybe it stops the noise from the room because they need to be focused. Probably they have practised a lot to be good at computer gaming. Perhaps they usually play every evening. I think now they are concentrating very hard and their fingers are moving very quickly. They want to beat the other people. I think they are probably very nervous. They want to be the best. I don't know if they get a prize for winning the competition. Perhaps the winner will go on to another competition. Usually you need to be very calm when you play games like this. That's hard when you are excited. I think these people are very excited too. Perhaps they are a little tired. Probably they have been playing for a long time and …

UNIT 11

Listening

EXAM PRACTICE

Ex 1a and 1c

Int. Good morning, Sadie. Thanks for joining us on Art Hour. You're a teacher at the Art Studio in the city's Glasson Museum. Can you tell us more about what your job entails?

S Sure. The Art Studio promotes the work of up-and-coming artists. I'm in charge of implementing free weekly art workshops related to the museum's exhibitions. I also visit schools to give specialist classes in certain techniques. It isn't that local art teachers don't know their stuff – they just don't have the amount of spare time they'd like to invest in researching the latest materials and techniques – whereas I can pass on knowledge from a great number of resources via the museum.

Int. Interesting. So, what skills are required for your job?

S It goes without saying you've got to be organised when half your day is spent going from one class to another. Now and then we have guest speakers, so one minute I'll be on the phone calling an illustrator to come and give a talk and the next I'll be planning a print-making session…

You can't overestimate the value of doing something you can't wait to get out of bed for – and no matter how hectic it gets there are no complaints from me.

Int. What are your goals as a teacher?

S I want to make new artists – some of whom haven't even picked up a paintbrush before – understand how art's developed through the ages, and to see that the art world is vibrant and active, and that anyone can have a go. There's a misconception that you can only become a successful artist if you go to art school but that isn't the case. I'll concede it might get your name out there a bit quicker because of the contacts you make along the way – but here at the museum, we can arrange exhibitions for our students which attract the press.

Int. Is your work as inspirational as it sounds?

S I hope so! One of the things I focus on is helping students explore the choices they make. When they finish a project, we discuss the decisions they made along the way. That provides a building block for the future – what worked, what didn't? What would they like to explore next? That's the way any new artist grows and increases their portfolio – not just of work but of techniques and ideas.

Int. How did you get into this line of work?

S I don't have any art or teaching qualifications. No one in my family was the least bit interested in art and neither was I – until I went along to a friend's degree exhibition. She'd done these massive canvasses covered in bright splashes of paint – I just didn't get the point, and we had a long discussion afterwards about what constitutes art and what doesn't. It got me thinking and I never stopped! My friend went on to launch a successful career as an artist.

Int. Is there anything listeners would find surprising about what you do?

S There's still this idea that museums are stuffy, formal places – and that deters some people from ever entering one. But museums are different places now to their counterparts of the past – though they may not all hold workshops in art. The point of mine is to get people moving around, getting their hands messy and just enjoying the process! The classes are full of energy and noise – I guess that's what takes most people aback when they pop in to have a look!

Int. How do you feel about your work as a whole?

S It's a great joy. I've wanted to guide people as artists and help them recognise their potential to create for a very long time. And now I have a platform to do that. I learn from students too – people have the most incredible minds and express themselves in a million different ways – it's almost as if art is a representation of humanity. That never fails to capture my imagination, and I know one day I'll see one of my students' work hanging in a national gallery!

Speaking

Ex 3c CD2 20

A For me, I think teachers have a very big influence on us. Do you agree?

B Oh yes. We spend a lot of time at school and when we're young we are influenced a lot by the people who talk to us. Teachers can influence the way we think about things because, of course, they tell us their opinions and when we're children we believe that that is right and often we grow up with the same ideas. Parents are very important but sometimes they influence us in a negative way. When I grew up my dad used to smoke and I hated the smell. So, when I was older I never wanted to start smoking. I guess that's a good negative influence …

Ex 3d CD2 21

A For me, I think teachers have a very big influence on us. Do you agree?

B Oh yes. We spend a lot of time at school and when we're young we are influenced a lot by the people who talk to us. Teachers can influence the way we think about things because, of course, they tell us their opinions and when we're children we believe that that is right and often we grow up with the same ideas. Parents are …

A Can I add something here? In my opinion teachers influence us a lot in deciding on a career too. They know what we're good at and they can give us ideas about directions we can take. Sometimes we respect our teachers so much that we want to be teachers too! What do you think?

B Yes, you're right. Also they show children what's right and wrong too – that's really important. Now, about parents. Obviously children copy their parents too, but sometimes they influence us in a negative way. When I grew up my dad used to smoke and I hated the smell. So, when I was older I never wanted to start smoking. I guess that's a good negative influence …

Ex 3e CD2 22

A OK, let's think about celebrities. Now, young people in particular look up to celebrities. They see talented people who are popular and earn a lot of money. They want to be like them. Everyone wants to be famous, don't they?

B Yeah – and they copy everything they do. Like the clothes they wear and their hairstyles!

A Sorry – I didn't catch that. What was that last thing you said?

B Sorry, 'hairstyles' – the way they do their hair – like shave it off or dye it lots of colours. Sometimes they even copy their behaviour. If a celebrity takes drugs, some kids might think that it's cool to do the same thing. That's not good.

A I completely agree with you. But sometimes celebrities can use their influence in a really positive way. Like some films stars talk a lot about poverty in some countries.

B Sorry – did you say – ponty?

A No, — poverty – people haven't got any money. Angelina Jolie has made a lot of people aware of that.

B Absolutely. They can make a real difference.

Unit 12

Listening

Ex 2

You will hear five short extracts in which people are talking about their diet. For questions 19–23, choose from the list (A–H) what each speaker wants to improve about their diet. Use the letters only once. There are three extra letters which you do not need to use.

Ex 3a

What mistakes does the nutritionist think people make when they eat out?

Ex 3b

M So, what do people tend to do wrong when they go out for dinner, for example?

F Good question. Well, it's easy to go 'Oh, I'm on a night out, it doesn't matter how much I eat' and then go ahead and order several courses. Of course you want to enjoy yourself, especially when you're paying for the meal, but it's not as challenging as you might think to eat healthily in restaurants. I'm not saying you should stick to salads, but fish, lean meats and vegetables are great choices – and tasty too!

Ex 5

Most people are aware of which foods they ought to avoid, but all of us at some point in our busy lives go straight to the prepared meals in the supermarket. I'd like to explain how to choose the best pre-packaged food.

Firstly, read the label. If it has ingredients you can't pronounce – leave it on the shelf. Chances are that the product is full of preservatives and other no-good fillers.

Second, test it. Some packaged foods can actually be pretty healthy. To sort out the good from the bad, ask yourself: Could I make this at home from the ingredients on the label? You can probably make some hummus, but not processed cheese – so forget the cheese!

Finally, pair it. What do I mean by this? Well, if you must have some of your favourites – like chicken nuggets or other processed meats – put it together with healthy sides, like carrot sticks or grapes.

EXAM PRACTICE

Part 1

M I don't know about you but when I'm busy I tend to either forget to eat or grab something as I'm rushing about – which usually ends up being something easy but not all that healthy – like sandwiches with a ton of mayonnaise on.

F It takes a lot of planning to avoid doing that, doesn't it? If I do think the night before about things I could take into work for lunch, I often find there's nothing in the fridge to make a decent snack from!

M And I know we're supposed to have an hour for lunch, but I rarely take that when I'm in the middle of something.

F I know.

Part 2

Most people are relatively aware of what they should and shouldn't eat – but there are definitely some myths surrounding certain foods. Some options you think are good for you have nutrition labels that are frankly terrifying! That's because they're full of the three scary Ss – sugar, saturated fat and salt – which can set you up for some serious health conditions such as high blood pressure, diabetes or heart disease.

Many of us are content to start the day with a bowl of cereal but the truth is that what's in most boxes in the cereal aisle isn't much better for you than what's in the cookie one. The sky-high sugar content is what's to blame. And then there's popcorn – considered a healthy alternative to crisps. But this is only the case when it's plain – preferably popped at home – and doesn't have a ton of fat on it, as it might at the cinema.

And then there are the things you believe to be bad for you, when in fact, you should probably be adding more of them to your diet. You'd probably think that guacamole for example, which contains lots of avocado, is too fatty, but you'd be wrong. Yes, there's a high calorie content, so you need to limit your intake, but actually, they can give you glowing skin and protect against cancer!

Part 3

S1 Do I eat a healthy balanced diet? Well, I try to! But like everyone I guess I do slip up in certain areas. It tends to be when I'm very hungry and need something quickly – or when I sit down in the evening in front of the television feeling a bit bored. I try to balance out the fatty things I love with fruit and green stuff, which I do also like, but I know I need to make more of an effort to eat more of the latter and less of the first. And I make an effort to sip water as I go through the day – sweet fizzy drinks have never been my thing.

S2 In the past I wouldn't drink anything but cola or fizzy orange drinks. These days I wouldn't be seen dead with a can of pop after a visit to the dentist led to a load of dental fillings! I still find it tricky cutting out the sweet stuff though – biscuits, cake, you name it, when there are machines selling it in the office. Other than that I think I eat pretty well – I limit my fat intake – though you do need some fats, which a lot of people overlook – it isn't all bad for you and it's worth finding out what's ok and what needs to be cut out altogether.

Part 4

Health education has to start in primary school for kids to grow up knowing what they should and shouldn't eat, and it's incredibly frustrating for nutritionists like me to discover that some schools still insist on offering unhealthy choices on the lunch menu. Burgers are still one of the most common things served up in school canteens. There may be healthy stuff there too, but what kid isn't going to choose those tasty things – especially if they aren't allowed them at home? Peanut butter sandwiches would actually be a better option, and yet people think they're just as bad for us as fries when they aren't.

Speaking

Part 1, Ex 1

OK, so, it was my mate's birthday and I invited her over for a meal. I decided to cook roast chicken so I went shopping and bought a chicken and lots of vegetables from my local supermarket. I put the chicken in the oven and then I peeled the potatoes and the carrots and I put the broccoli into a pan of water. I then boiled the carrots for ten minutes and while I was doing that, I checked the chicken and .....

Int. Thank you.

Part 2, Ex 1 CD2 29

A In the first picture I can see some chefs and they are preparing food in a kitchen. I think it is a professional kitchen. There are a lot of chefs and they are all busy cooking. I can see seven chefs. The chef at the front is cooking something very hot. There are flames coming from his pan. But he doesn't seem worried. Perhaps it is part of the cooking method. It is a big kitchen, so it's probably a big restaurant. I like this picture. The second picture is of a man in a kitchen with his children. He is holding his young child and at the same time he is checking his phone. His little girl is doing something, maybe washing or cutting some fruit. She is making a mess. The man isn't watching her. I don't like fruit so I like the first picture more I think.

Int. Max, do you enjoy cooking?

M Yes.

Part 3, Ex 1

A OK, I'll start. It's good to eat in a school canteen because it's easy to get to and it doesn't cost much. But sometimes the food isn't well-cooked and it can be a bit boring. It's also very noisy in a canteen. Also you see always the same people. Also, sometimes there's a long queue because there are lots of people who want to eat.

B Now it's my turn. It's good to eat in a fast food restaurant. I really like burgers and chicken with chips. It's very tasty. Sometimes I go at lunchtime with my friends. There are lots of fast food restaurants near my work. We often go to a burger restaurant and I always order a cheese burger with fries.

A Now it's my turn. It's good to go on a picnic...

Part 3, Ex 2 CD2 31

A I think the canteen is popular because the people don't have a choice.

B I think the fast food restaurant is popular because the food is good.

Part 4, Ex 1 CD2 32

A That's an interesting question. Today a lot of families don't eat together and I think that's a pity. It's important because …

B I agree. In my family we always eat dinner together. Well, maybe not always, sometimes my dad finishes work late and so we go ahead without him. But it's a good opportunity to

A Yes. It's a time when you can talk over what you've done during the day and …

B As I was saying, it's a good opportunity to talk about any problems …

Int. Thank you.

PRACTICE TEST

Part 1

1

M Hi! Did you catch the second part of the new TV drama series last night?

F Oh, yes. I saw the first episode last week and I was intrigued to see what happened.

M Me too. I loved it. I thought the ending was very clever. It's difficult to follow on from a great opening like last week's, but I think it definitely succeeded.

F It certainly kept your attention and the acting was superb. It was maybe a little overcomplicated for me. I wasn't too sure who actually committed the crime in the end.

M I've got the book – it isn't as interesting as the series but it might help.

2 Hi Megan, it's me, Rob. I feel really bad about missing you at lunch yesterday – I thought I'd be able to get there by one-thirty but we had a mini crisis at work and I couldn't leave until half past two and then I knew it was too late because your lectures start at three. So could you maybe fit in dinner this week sometime? I'm free Wednesday and Thursday and finish work at six. We've got a lot of catching up to do and I want to make up for missing you yesterday. So it will be on me. OK? Let me know. See you!

3 I was delighted to receive the Writers Prize in March. It's wonderful to know that others appreciate what you've done – and to make you a winner! And that in spite of my doubts about my ability all through the writing process! The Dark Angel is my first book and it took me over three years to write but I was lucky to be working mornings only and able to fit in my writing in the afternoon. I guess my main advice to new writers is to find the time to write every day and check out all your facts well before you start writing. Someone is bound to spot mistakes!

4

M I hear you went to Paris for the weekend?

F Yes – thanks for the hotel recommendation. It was just right. We'd never have found it ourselves.

M We appreciated the lack of noise, which is surprising in such a central location.

F Absolutely – and the food was of a really high standard, although I must say I wish they'd serve breakfast a little longer.

M I know! We were too late every morning and missed it. One thing we noticed – the room was a bit cold. Was yours?

F Actually I prefer cooler rooms – especially as it was so hot outside when we were there.

5 The Gateway Festival is a popular open-air music event for several reasons. Big attractions are that it is free for local residents and also gives local musicians an opportunity to perform and perhaps attract useful contacts and agents. It's therefore difficult to understand the council's recent decision to stop funding the festival. Their reasoning is that they need to cut their spending budgets. However, the festival actually brings in money through ticket sales outside the locality, and from the selling of souvenirs and clothes – and in fact it makes a small profit each year. The council's choice is more likely due to complaints about the mess left that is usually left behind.

6 You know, it seems that one of the best forms of crime prevention is really very simple – it's making people feel as if they're being watched! You probably thinking I'm talking about security cameras but no, I'm referring to a method used recently to combat bike theft. A poster of two staring eyes was placed near the bikes and remarkably the thefts dropped by fifty percent. It taps into a natural fear of being watched and makes thieves think twice! There aren't any statistics to tell us whether the thieves just move on to another bike rack yet though!

7

F I'm glad I went to that lecture. Professor Jenner's a very good speaker.

M Yes. He knows how to engage an audience. His stories about his trips to the Arctic were hilarious!

F And at the same time, very interesting. The places he's mentioned – it's made me want to read up more about it.

M I'm glad our next assignment isn't due in for a week though. I've got so much on at the moment.

F Yes, but I'm looking forward to doing it and I definitely can't wait until his next lecture.

8M Hi! I'm waiting for Brad. We're just off to watch the evening match in town. Aren't you going?

F Yeah – I was planning to but didn't you get a text? There's been a problem at the football ground. Something about some seating that's collapsed I think – something to do with last week's storms. So, the match isn't happening I'm afraid.

M I'm glad it was empty if that happened. So, when is it going to be played? Next week?

F Apparently it's not. Everyone's getting a refund on their tickets – office staff are sorting it out now.

M Oh no. That's a pain. I was really looking forward to it.

Part 2

It's a real pleasure to be here at Northlands School, talking to you about my acting career. As you may know I was a student here myself eight years ago! I have great memories of the place. It was here that I had my first experience on a stage. My English teacher was putting on a play, and it was actually my History teacher, Miss Turner, who encouraged me to audition for the school play because I loved reading stuff out in class. Well, I got the leading role! I'm grateful to have had that opportunity because an agent gave me my first job after seeing me perform in the same play when I was at drama college. So this is where it all began!

I think it's essential to take an acting course if you want to learn the skills you need to become a good actor. You learn more than just the differences between stage or TV acting –an actor needs to know about the technical side of things too, such as lighting. Even learning a bit about costume design is more useful than you'd think.

A good actor must be a good observer. To be able to play a range of different characters the actor must watch people everywhere and remember how they look, walk and talk. I remember I once played a female politician and although I've seen countless numbers of them on TV, I based my character on one I recognised sitting on an Underground train once!

My parents were concerned when I got my first part in a film at the age of 21. They'd expected me to be playing a student or something and they thought that I wasn't experienced enough to play someone's stepmother! But plenty of actors take on mature parts at a young age. It's great to have as much life experience as possible but if opportunities come, we need to take them. That in itself is part of your experience.

I had to travel to the other side of the world for my first film, to Australia, and spend six months away. I thought I might be a bit nervous when it came to leaving home. In fact I was surprisingly calm – I was about to embark on an exciting adventure. I learned so much from acting with other talented professionals and this undoubtedly helped me go further in my career. Of course while I was there I did a bit more than just act every day – I got involved in a few sports, too. I went surfing, which was amazing, but the highlight was when I went diving, which enabled me to explore the incredible coral reefs.

When I returned to the UK, I auditioned for various parts in TV series. The one I really hoped I'd get was in my favourite crime series – so when I landed a part in a TV comedy series I was pretty surprised – I hadn't thought I'd get anything like that. I suppose I saw myself as a more serious kind of actor – someone who'd be in mysteries or action adventures perhaps.

All this brings me up to the present. I've just finished another film and then I'm going on tour in the UK for the first time as a professional stage actor. I turned down a part in a play called Snow White to be in one called The Corridor, which is more, what I'd call a 'meaty' part – there's more to get my teeth into as a serious actor. We'll be here in September – come and see us if you can, it's a great play!

So, if you want to follow your dream of becoming an actor, my advice is to get experience wherever you can. It's tricky when you're starting out to get on a film set even for local TV stations – but there are sometimes opportunities to volunteer at a theatre near you – even if you're just tidying away the props or selling tickets. It's a great way to find out how everything works. Good luck!

Part 3 🎧 CD2 35

1 I always found history a bit dull at school and consequently I didn't do particularly well in it. It wasn't that I had no interest – I think maybe it was the way the classes were delivered. Anyway, I've gone back to do classes in the evenings after work and what a difference! It's almost as if characters from the past are in the room with us. That goes to show what a difference the teaching makes. There aren't that many options for careers in history, and to be honest, I probably wouldn't have gone into the field anyway, but I'm really glad I've gone back to it this way.

2 When I go abroad I can sit there all day listening to people chatting in their own languages. It's fascinating and I love to try and tune in to what they're saying. Anyway, that's why I'm doing a course in Japanese – maybe I'll find out more about Japan, too. We've got a brilliant teacher who makes the classes fun, though it's slow progress and tough to get your head round the written characters. Languages aren't really my strong point, but I like the way studying them makes me use my brain! I'll probably never actually get to use what I'm learning outside the classroom, but that's OK.

3 When I say I'm doing a degree in physics, people seem to either look horrified or impressed! It's got a reputation for being tough, hasn't it? I suppose it's because it involves a lot of maths, which some people aren't confident about. I love it, though. I've always had an enquiring mind and I feel like I'm finding out something new every day. It answers a lot of questions I had as a kid – stuff my parents couldn't answer for me. There are loads of things you can go on to do with a degree in physics. I probably won't go on and use physics afterwards – I just love studying it!

4 What do I like about studying geography? I get asked that question a lot. The second question I get asked is 'So, are you going to travel the world?' Well, of course I like finding out about other cultures and places and people – who doesn't? But there's no need to study geography to do that – anyone can get on a plane. The thing is, if you study geography, you really look deeply at the way humans interact with the environment, and that can inform the way governments do things – in order to make our world a better place to live. There's real, practical value in that – that's what I love.

5 I've just enrolled in a philosophy course. I didn't have the option of doing anything like that at school, so I'm finding it really interesting. I used to think it was all about discussing the meaning of life and that kind of thing but there's much more to it than that. We're encouraged to speak up and voice our opinions in class – something I found difficult at first cos I didn't want people to disagree with me! But, actually, one person's view point is as valid as anyone else's, and now I feel much more sure of myself. You never know, it may help me in meetings at work, too.

Part 4

F Good morning, Andy and thanks for joining us today on Culture Time. As a culture and technology expert you're here to talk to us about symbols called 'emojis' which are used in emails and text messages. How did it all start?

M Firstly, as you know, emojis are little digital pictures which are used to express ideas or emotions in electronic communication – like smiley or sad faces to indicate happiness or sadness. Nowadays there are literally hundreds of them, with variations depending on the technology you use. But even in the 1990s when they first appeared in Japan, they were an instant hit with teenagers. Now everyone's using them – I'm sure the inventors had no idea that the icons would end up being used on a global scale!

F Does using emojis have a negative effect on our language skills?

M Actually, they can add an extra layer of meaning to our communication and make it richer. Some people are of the opinion that using pictures instead of words all the time 'dumbs down' our language skills – you know, makes us less capable of expressing ourselves well, especially in writing. In fact, emojis engage the part of your brain which uses symbolic and visual thinking – and they also have the potential to break down language barriers.

F How do people use emojis?

M People are really inventive with them – why tell your friend you're on the way to her house when you can send an illustration of a car, a clock and a house? They can be like fun puzzles. They can also be used to indicate how the recipient should react – like, if you put a smile at the end of a sentence, it's telling them they should have laughed at it. I guess you could say the usage of emojis is as individual as the people sending them, which is what's really fascinating for me.

F Do you use emojis – and if so, how?

M I do. I use them in conventional ways – like to show I'm having a cup of coffee or whatever – providing the picture exists in the first place – which they don't always. My friend always ends her messages with a picture of a horse's head. It reminds me of a funny conversation we had once. No one else understands the reference, so it makes me feel closer to her – I really appreciate that. Sometimes I try to use unusual icons in my messages – just to make things interesting! People respond in funny ways.

F How effective do you think emojis are in expressing emotion?

M Sometimes you aren't just feeling happy or sad – which were all we were able to express in the early days of emojis. These days you can say all sorts – feeling angry, surprised, whatever... My daughter and her friends use a picture of a ghost if they're feeling a bit fed up and they send back pictures of things like cute animals to cheer each other up. Everyone has their own codes no matter what age they are.

F Do you think emojis can ever be confusing?

M There's often a bit of ambiguity in electronic communication – especially in texts – because you can't hear the tone of the person's voice like you would face-to-face. It's why people might end up feeling angry or confused because they've misunderstood the message. I suppose if I were to give any advice, I'd say choose your pictures carefully – one or two used appropriately can make sure recipients get the meaning that was intended.

F Why do you think people have adopted emojis so completely?

M Good question! In some ways using pictures is a kind of shorthand – there isn't as much effort required as writing long sentences. And the same symbol can be understood by people of many different languages across the world. For me I think it's because emojis can be like a smile for a colleague across the room, or the small talk you make when getting a coffee – you can stay connected to others, even when there's nothing specific to communicate. They bring fun into everyday life.

Unit 1

Listening

1 Students' answers

2 Students' answers

3a 1 multiple choice **2** sentence completion **3** multiple matching **4** multiple choice

b Students' answers

4a B

b No, the speaker does not mention concern, regret or anger. The following words and phrases are used: I should have…, I start to wish…

5a 1 blink **2** sleep

b the effect of Smartphones on eyesight; **1** eye problems **2** over-exposure

6a D

b we're missing out on opportunities to appreciate the world around us – that's what really gets to me, people walking about, heads down, staring at screens; all of them

7a 3

b A

8 Students' answers

EXAM PRACTICE

1 1 C **2** B **3** A

2 Students' answers

Speaking

1 Students' answers

2 Students' answers

3 a F — only personal questions **b** F not discussion **c** T **d** F not too short **e** T **f** F shouldn't need to speculate

4a Do you do sport regularly?

b C gives a good answer. A is too short. B includes a lot of basic mistakes. D is too long. E is a prepared answer, not relevant.

EXAM PRACTICE

1 Students' answers

Unit 2

Listening

1 & 2 Students' answers

EXAM PRACTICE 1

1a **Speaker 1** optimistic; **Speaker 2** optimistic; **Speaker 3** pessimistic

b Speaker 1 is the most realistic because, although he thinks he has a good chance of getting into the university of his choice, he is also making back-up plans. Students' answers for second and third bullet point.

2 Positive feelings: amused, enthusiastic, cheerful, secure, relieved; Negative feelings: concerned, impatient, uneasy, furious, suspicious, dissatisfied

3a 1 disappointed **2** annoyed **3** grateful

b 1 b **2** c **3** a

EXAM PRACTICE 2

1c

2a The speaker gave some advice. ☐

b The speaker talked about their feelings. ☑

c The speaker received advice from someone. ☑

d The speaker might have changed their opinion. ☑

e The speaker was given two pieces of advice. ☐

3 Students' answers

4 **S1** c **S2** d **S3** a

5 Students' answers

Speaking

EXAM PRACTICE 1

1a & b Students' answers

c present simple: both photographs show
present continuous: the men are wearing clothes
present perfect simple: they've done something difficult
present perfect continuous: the men have been playing football

d 1 show **2** all **3** both **4** whereas **5** however **6** too **7** while **8** but **9** main **10** whereas

e Suggested answers:
a In both photographs the men are quite young.

b In photograph 1 it looks very quiet but in photograph 2 it's probably very noisy.

c The men in both photographs are probably very tired.

d The climber is very fit and the footballers are fit too.

EXAM PRACTICE 2

1 Students' answers

2 Students' answers

Unit 3

Listening

1 Students' answers

2a **a** F **b** I **c** F/N **d** N **e** F/N **f** I **g** F **h** F/N

b **1** c **2** b **3** h **4** a

3a **5** I **6** N **7** I **8** F/N

b **5** friends, somewhere informal, they are talking about an article they have read about CCTV
6 a teacher and a student, in class, a debate about the pros and cons of CCTV
7 friends / colleagues, somewhere informal, they are talking about CCTV in a negative way
8 a teacher, in class, giving a homework assignment about crime prevention

4 **1** no opinion **2** no opinion **3** in favour **4** no opinion **5** no opinion **6** against **7** against **8** no opinion

5 Students' answers

EXAM PRACTICE

1 Students' answers

2a **1** probably formal **2** probably formal / neutral **3** probably informal **4** probably formal / neutral

b **1** B **2** B **3** C **4** A

3 Students' answers

Speaking

1 Students' answers

2 Students' answers

3a Students' answers

b **a** They didn't talk about smoking and driving fast. **b** Students' answers **c** They did interact.

c **a** have **b** with **c** place **d** think **e** completely **f** about **g** feel **h** right **i** view **j** agree **k** partly **l** opinion **m** still **n** move **o** views

d **Organising the discussion**: 1 2 3 6 14

Asking for opinion: 4 7 9 10

Giving opinion: 5 8 11 12 13 15

e Students' answers

EXAM PRACTICE

1 Students' answers.

Unit 4

Listening

1 Students' answers

2a & b **Agreeing**
Tell me about it! S
You've got a point. M
Absolutely! S
I couldn't agree more. S
I guess so. W
Disagreeing
I'm not sure I'm with you there. M
We'll have to agree to disagree. S
I don't know about that. M
That's not necessarily the case. M
I don't think so. S

3a Students' answers

4a Students' answers

b That's for sure! (agreement); Totally! (agreement); I was just going to say that! (agreement); Yeah, I did. (agreement)

5a They agree.

b after someone expresses an opinion

c

F What do you reckon about those people who do, like, a hundred marathons in a year or something silly like that – in order to raise money for charity?

M Erm, I don't know, really. I mean, are they doing it for themselves so they look good or genuinely doing it to help other people?

F What does it matter? I suppose if someone's benefitting through someone else giving up their time to help out or take part in challenges or even just make a donation – I can't see the problem in that.

M Sure – though I bet most people wouldn't do something they really hated for the sake of others.

F Probably not!

6 Students' answers

7 **a** agree **b** agree **c** agree **d** disagree **e** disagree

8 **1**, **2** and **4** are agreement / disagreement questions.

EXAM PRACTICE

1 **1** C **2** B **3** C

2 Students' answers

Speaking

1 Students' answers

2 Students' answers

3 **1** C **2** A **3** B **4** E **5** D

4 **a** his family moved to France when he was 11

b his dad had a job there

c it was hard to keep in touch with friends / he became good at French

b **a** he needs more exercise because he's too lazy
b go to the gym / for a swim / he uses his car too much / watches TV
c today everyone's tempted to chill out because they work very hard and there's a lot of interesting entertainment on TV etc.

c **a** because of   **b** worst thing   **c** big benefit
d for example   **e** like   **f** for instance   **g** such as

5   Students' answers

EXAM PRACTICE

1   Students' answers.

Unit 5

Listening

1   Students' answers. The musicians / composers shown are Drake, Mozart, Orbital, Taylor Swift, Bob Marley and Ed Sheeran.

2a   Students' answers

b **a** uncombed   **b** iron   **c** millionaire

c **1** c   **2** b   **3** a

3a   **a** believe   **b** programme   **c** be impressed

b A

c No, because they were not part of the answer.

4a   C

b **a** a lot   **b** to sell something in a group of people to the person who promises to pay the highest price
c untidy, dirty   **d** normal, ordinary. You needed to understand 'down to earth' and 'scruffy'.

c Students' answers

d Students' answers

EXAM PRACTICE

1   **1** C   **2** A   **3** B

2   Students' answers

Speaking

1   Students' answers

2   No. She doesn't talk about whether candidates only talk about their own photographs or not.

3a   'Compare the photographs and say why the people have chosen to listen to music in these places.'

b He doesn't answer the question. He says which photograph he prefers.

c Students' answers

4   Students' answers

5   **1** After one candidate has talked for a minute the other candidate is asked a question about their partner's photographs.   **2** You need to extend your answer.
3 It's a personal question.

6   Students' answers

EXAM PRACTICE

1   Students' answers

2   Students' answers

Unit 6

Listening

1   Students' answers

2a   Students' answers

b C

c a

3a   a

b b

4   **a** opinion   **b** agreement   **c** feeling   **d** attitude

5   A

6a   3 is a gist question, 4 is a detail question

b gist, detail

7   3B, 4C

8   All of them should be ticked.

EXAM PRACTICE

1a   **1** B   **2** A   **3** A   **4** C

b **1** agreement   **2** feeling   **3** attitude   **4** opinion

c robotic fish, water catcher, robot crab, robot snake

2   Students' answers

Speaking

1   Students' answers

3a   Students' answers

b **A** 1 type / 2 in   **B** 3 word / 4 when   **C** 5 thingummy / 6 exact   **D** 7 call   **E** 8 for / 9 same   **F** 10 what / 11 gone

c **Explain the problem:**

what do you call that ...?
sorry, it's gone
I used to know the word for this ...
Oh, what is it?
I don't know the name in English ...
What's the word?
I can't remember the exact word ...

Say it in other words:

it's the same thing that …
it's a special type of …
it's when it runs round …
it's a thingummy …

EXAM PRACTICE

1 Students answers

2 Students' answers

Unit 7

Listening

1 Students' answers

2a Students' answers

b **1** society **2** attention

c Students' answers

3a **a** a place **b** a vowel **c** a noun; students' answers
d students' answers; adjective **e** students' answers
f a feeling / attitude / opinion; an adjective

b **a** online **b** event **c** previews **d** fashion **e** windows
f passionate

c Students' answers

EXAM PRACTICE

1a **1** Norway **2** design **3** models **4** celebrities
5 identify **6** complaints **7** social media

b & c Students' answers

2 Students' answers

Speaking

1 Students' answers

2 Students' answers

3 Students' answers

4 Students' answers

5a Students' answers

b **1** look **2** it looks as if **3** could **4** guess
5 maybe **6** could well **7** I would say **8** There's
another possibility. **9** might

EXAM PRACTICE

1 Students' answers

Unit 8

Listening

1 **1** b **2** a **3** a **4** b **5** a **6** a

2 All of them!

3 Students' answers

5 Correct spelling: **b d f**. Corrected spelling: **a** achievement
c piece **e** receive

6a **a** acceptable **b** desirable **c** incredible **d** adaptable
e believable **f** responsible

b **a** -able **b** -able **c** -ible

7 **a** all **b** creation (from create), education (from educate)
c collection (after c), reception (after p)

8a **1** a noun b adj c adj d-f nouns
2 the word in sentence 2 (the article 'a' tell us this)

b **a** ceiling **b** professional **c** acceptable **d** business
e permission **f** ambition

EXAM PRACTICE

1 Students' answers

2 **1** colleagues **2** inspiration **3** environmental
4 unforgettable **5** incredible **6** valuable **7** request
8 passion **9** confidence **10** achievements

3 Students' answers

Speaking

1 **a** 5 **b** 3 minutes

2a & b Students' answers

3a Students' answers

b **a** about 25 seconds **b** yes **c** yes **d** no **e** no
f important

c Students' answers

d **a** Students' answers **b** 1 'it would be good … but it's
not vital' 'it makes a lot of difference' 'it's essential'

EXAM PRACTICE

1 Students' answers

2 Students' answers

Unit 9

Listening

1 Students' answers

2 2

3 **Speaker 1** c **Speaker 2** a **Speaker 3** b

4a **Speaker 1** Do the most difficult tasks first.
Speaker 2 Cut out unnecessary activities.
Speaker 3 Make a to-do list.

b Students' answers

EXAM PRACTICE

1 Students' answers

2a **Speaker 1** E and H **Speaker 2** A and C
Speaker 3 F and B **Speaker 4** D and C
Speaker 5 H and G

b You will hear five people talking about time management techniques. Choose <u>the strategy each person adopted to help them</u> manage their time more effectively.

c **Speaker 1** H   **Speaker 2** A   **Speaker 3** F
  Speaker 4 D   **Speaker 5** G

d Students' answers

3 Students' answers

Speaking

1-3 Students' answers

4a **a** all options   **b** having fun

b **a** tricky   **b** depends   **c** suppose   **d** mean   **e** point
  f too   **g** might   **h** for   **i** as we said   **j** completely
  k more   **l** true   **m** persuaded   **n** go

5 **a** The most important thing is   **b** Top of the list is…
  c That's nowhere near as important as   **d** I think the
  majority of people would say that   **e** It's way more
  important than   **f** It's easy to see the least important

EXAM PRACTICE

Students' answers

Unit 10

Listening

1 Students' answers

2a **1** a   **2** b

b **a** detail   **b** gist

3b a detail. There is no reference to opinion in the
  question and the options are factual.

c C

d All of it!

4b **a** Question 2   **b** Question 1   **c** Question 3

c **1** Question 3   **2** Question 2   **3** Question 1

EXAM PRACTICE

1a **1** A   **2** B   **3** A

2 Students' answers

Speaking

1 Students' answers

2 Students' answers

3a Candidate A: 41 seconds
  Candidate B: 1 minute 10 seconds

b Students' answers

c Suggested answers:

  In both photographs people are playing computer games
  competitively. *However*, they are in different places *and*
  they are competing for different reasons. In the first

picture it's a big competition *which* is in a big room and
there are lots of people playing at the same time. *In
contrast to this*, in the second picture there are *only* two
people playing *and* they are at home in a living room.
I think they're friends *and* it's probably a friendly game
where the winner is not important *whereas* in the first
picture they all want to win the competition.

d Students' answers

EXAM PRACTICE

1 Students' answers

2 Students' answers

Unit 11

Listening

1 Students' answers

2 Students' answers

3a-d Students' answers

e **a** Q6   **b** Q3   **c** Q7   **d** Q1   **e** Q5   **f** Q5   **g** Q2

4a **a** Q4   **b** Q2   **c** Q7   **d** Q3   **e** Q6   **f** Q1   **g** Q5

EXAM PRACTICE

1a **1** C   **2** C   **3** A   **4** C   **5** B   **6** B   **7** A

b **a** N   **b** Y   **c** N

Speaking

1 Students' answers

2 Students' answers

3a & b Students' answers

c Candidate B talks too much, dominates.

d Candidate A interrupts politely : Can I add…?

e Candidate A doesn't understand some words (hairstyle /
  poverty) and asks for clarification. Candidate B clarifies by
  glossing the words and speaks more clearly.

EXAM PRACTICE

1 Students' answers

Unit 12

Listening

1 Students' answers

2 b

3a Students' answers

b B

4 **1** b   **2** c   **3** a

5 Students' answers

6 Students' answers

EXAM PRACTICE

Part 1

C

Part 2

1 Myths **2** cookie **3** calorie

Part 3

Speaker 1 A, **Speaker 2** B

Part 4

A

Speaking
EXAM PRACTICE

Part 1

1 She goes into too much detail.

2 Students' answers

Part 2

1 **A** describes both pictures in detail, doesn't compare and doesn't answer the question. **B** answers with just one word.

Part 3

1 They take turns and don't have a conversation. They don't ask for and give opinions, they don't talk about the same options but different ones, they don't interact. **B** doesn't actually answer the question but talks about his own preference. They repeat the same phrases. 'it's good to eat…' **B** repeats 'also' several times.

2 They give one sentence about their own opinion. They don't interact or discuss, they don't expand.

3 Students' answers

Part 4

1 They interrupt each other without giving their partner time to finish a sentence or develop an idea.

2 Students' answers

Practice test

Part 1

1 B **2** C **3** B **4** C **5** B **6** C **7** B **8** A

Part 2

9 History teacher   **10** (drama) college   **11** lighting

12 an underground train   **13** step(-)mothe   **14** calm

15 diving   **16** comedy   **17** The Corridor   **18** theatre

Part 3

19 D   **20** E   **21** B   **22** F   **23** G

Part 4

24 B   **25** C   **26** C   **27** A   **28** B   **29** A   **30** B

SCHOLASTIC LTD.

Euston House

24 Eversholt Street

London

NW1 1DB

Publisher: Jacquie Bloese

Senior Development Editor: Sarah Silver

Editor: Amanda Anderson

Designer: Mo Choy

Cover design: Nicolle Thomas

Photo research: Pupak Navabpour

Photo credits:

Cover M. Van Caspel/iStockphoto

Unit 1 Piranka, Highwaystarz, Stockphoto4u, M. Van Caspel, simonkr, Pixel Embargo, RoBeDeRo, W. Smahar/iStockphoto; U. Baumgarten, Popperfoto/Getty Images; Photodisc. **Unit 2** PeopleImages, Z. Zeremski, digitalskillet, E. Kondoros, M. Van Caspel, blyjak, J. Snyder, andresr, londoneye, People Images/iStockphoto; M. Powell, M. Kolbe/Getty Images. **Unit 3** J. Morgan/Alamy; L. Neal/AFP, Barcroft Media, China Foto Press/Getty Images; i-Stockr, Ed Stock, M. Krakowiak, E. Hart, J. Bryson, M. Van Caspel/iStockphoto; T. White/Reuters. **Unit 4** Machine Headz, C. Okada, C. Philip, M. Van Caspel, B. McIlhargey/iStockphoto; T. Vine/Superstock. **Unit 5** T. Whitby, M. Tullberg, Imagno, M. Metcalfe, C. Walter, T. Wargo, J. Finney/Getty Images; Arctic Images/Corbis; M. Van Caspel, zodebala, energyy, Neustockimages, andresr, Lighthousebay/iStockphoto. **Unit 6** A. Dennis/AFP, S. Abdullah, C. Sung-Jun/Getty Images; M. Bazo/Reuters; G. Murdoch; E. Lam, M. Van Caspel, druvo, Rawpixel Ltd, Avid Creative Inc, simonkr/iStockphoto; FPW/Alamy; Blend Images/Superstock. **Unit 7** S. Granitz, M. Flokis/Getty Images; R. Herret/Alamy; M. Van Caspel, gpointstudio, digitalskillet, urbancow, A. Krauchuk, S. Debenport, Foto Speedy, Möner, S. Chiang, shalamov, P. Vuckovic/iStockphoto. **Unit 8** Ananaline, P. Steib, M. Van Caspel, N. Venturin, F. Corticchia, P. Hadzinski, rilueda/iStockphoto; vector-RGB/Shutterstock. **Unit 9** Lesia_G, I. Balasanov, L. Konuk, M. Van Caspel, serezniy, Rapid Eye, svetikd, People Images, F. Bacci, 123 foto, chrisdorney/iStockphoto. **Unit 10** EA Games; Minecraft; M. Van Caspel, vadimguzhva/iStockphoto; R. Beck, J. Mambromata/AFP, T. Szczerbowski, R. Gilmore/Getty Images; OJO Images/Superstock. **Unit 11** Photofusion, S. Platt, M. Ngan/Getty Images; double_p, Leaf, Juanmonino, M. Van Caspel, S. Chiang, Yuri, Braun S, 4x6, oversnap/iStockphoto. **Unit 12** J. Chio, Peteer S, S. Debenport, C. Futcher, J. Doly/iStockphoto; B. Hustace/Corbis; Hero Images/Getty Images. **Practice Test** Big Shots, M. Heffernann, M. Harrington/Getty Images; Superstock.

Cartoons (pages 32 and 49) by Gray Jolliffe/Illustration Ltd

The publishers would like to acknowledge the following source materials:

Unit 1 'Are Smartphones Making Us Stupid?' from Scholastic Choices Magazine, September 2014 'Hefty Texting' from Scholastic Science World Magazine, February 2015 'Icy Impact' from Scholastic Science World Magazine, December 2014 **Unit 2** 'The Science of Optimism' from Scholastic Choices Magazine, January 2015 **Unit 6** 'Inspired by Nature' from Scholastic Scienceworld Magzine, December 2014 **Unit 8** 'Dream Jobs' from Scholastic Choices Magazine, November/December 2014 **Unit 9** 'Beat the Clock' from Scholastic Choices Magazine, September 2014 **Unit 11** 'Inspiring Young Artists' from Scholastic Art Magzine, February 2014 **Unit 12** 'Foods Every Teen Should Eat' from Scholastic Choices Magazine, September 2013 '10 Worst Foods for Teens' from Scholastic Choices Magazine, October 2013

Printed in Italy